T0077903

Sparks of Courage

KASY HEART

WESTBOW
PRESS®
A DIVISION OF THOMAS NELSON
& ZONDERVAN

Scripture quotations marked (NIV) are taken from the Holy Bible, New International Version®, NIV®. Copyright © 1973, 1978, 1984, 2011 by Biblica, Inc.™ Used by permission of Zondervan. All rights reserved worldwide. www. zondervan.com The "NIV" and "New International Version" are trademarks registered in the United States Patent and Trademark Office by Biblica, Inc.™

The Holy Bible, English Standard Version® (ESV®)
Copyright © 2001 by Crossway,
a publishing ministry of Good News Publishers.
All rights reserved.
ESV Text Edition: 2016

WestBow Press books may be ordered through booksellers or by contacting:

WestBow Press
A Division of Thomas Nelson & Zondervan
1663 Liberty Drive
Bloomington, IN 47403
www.westbowpress.com
1 (866) 928-1240

ISBN: 978-1-9736-0481-5 (sc)
ISBN: 978-1-9736-0480-8 (hc)
ISBN: 978-1-9736-0482-2 (e)

Library of Congress Control Number: 2017915867

Print information available on the last page.

WestBow Press rev. date: 11/08/2017

I dedicate this book to God.

I dedicate this book to my parents.

I dedicate this book to my children, God-
children, and grandchildren.

I dedicate this book to my two awesome sisters.

I dedicate this book to my awesome
brother and my sister-in-law.

Lastly, I dedicate this book to all my nieces and nephews.

Contents

Preface

AS I BATTLED DOMESTIC VIOLENCE FOR TOO MANY years, I did not know if I would see the next day. The physical and mental abuse tortured me, but the depression, lack of courage, and the deceiving lies of the enemy had me captive.

"My life was a prison. There were many people that asked me: Why don't I leave him? They would say to me I was so stupid. And I remember crying myself to sleep asking myself the same question: "Why can't I leave him?"

"... Depression overtook my life. The lies of the enemy were blinding me in leading me to believe that I never even needed the Lord Jesus. I felt multiple bricks attaching to my body, and one by one the weight of the bricks made it difficult for me to stand tall with my head lifted high; each brick had a name ..."

"The devil was following me wherever I went, and yes, the devil was having a blazing blast twisting my loneliness ..."

God has led me to write my testimony so that you can understand that because of my ignorance of my own identity and self-worth, the deceiving lies of the devil grounded dark roots in my soul. I was blind to see the truth of God's purpose for my life. And yes, I want to say if I could do things different, I would, but I also see that if it had not been for my trails, I would not have written this book. It is written, "Go home to your friends and tell them how much the Lord has done for you, and how he has had mercy on you" (Mark 5:19 ESV), and "If I alone bear witness about myself, my testimony is not deemed true" (John 5:31 ESV).

I am now a Christian, and though there will be disagreements to what I believe, I have been given boldness to speak. There are many reasons for a relationship to be abusive. I will list a few:

*The relationship lacks the foundation in the Lord Jesus.
*One or both partners have identity, painful, and insecurity trauma.
*The spouses' childhood lacked nurturing or caused negative learned behavior.
*The husband and wife are in denial to seek marriage counseling and mental health therapy.
*There is a lack of Respect and Love with in the married couple.
*One or both partners have an uncontrolled alcohol usage combined with unresolved emotions.
*Silence from one of the partners.

I believe that no one should remain in a physical or mental abusive relationship whether they are Christian or not. Again, this is my belief. Yes, the vow says till death do you apart, but I have also read that the man should be an example of a righteous husband in the home by showing the Lord Jesus' love. It is written, "In this same way, husbands should love their wives as their own bodies. He who loves his wife loves himself" (Ephesians 5:28 ESV). Here it is, husbands that beat or mentally abuse their wives do not love themselves, so how can they show their wives love!

There needs to be a true Lord guided balance in the

relationship: A wife needs to Love and Respect her husband! And a husband needs to Love and Respect his wife! When a husband or wife cannot love and respect themselves, they will not be able to love and respect their spouse.

The resources that inspired me through my writing have been the Holy Bible, Father God, the Lord Jesus, and my personal experiences.

My real life story is structured chronologically and begins when I get married. At the end of every chapter, I write highlights on what I have learned from my life's experiences with connection to God's Holy Word. Sparks of Courage from the Lord gathered and led me to act.

Have there been any challenges in writing my real life story? I will say that any of the eight dimensions of wellness: financial, intellectual, vocational, social, physical, environmental, spiritual, and emotional have detoured me away from writing at one time or another. However, I will highlight the emotional challenges on where to begin and when to end this book: It has taken me about two years to write this portion of my life, and the reason was not related to remembering my past. One of my challenges was the feeling of being overwhelmed because I had so much to write, so I had to decide on a word count goal, and a beginning and ending point of my real life story.

Another challenge was silencing the negative thoughts of not being a good writer and that no one would read my real life story. The continued challenge was the emotional pain that resurfaced as I wrote details to the abuse I endured, and the repeated healing process I followed with my Wellness tools, therapy, Certified Peer Specialist trainings, and daily prayer with my Lord Jesus. After healing process mentioned above, emotional triggers were no longer a hidden secret allowing me to refocus to the Lord's truth in my life for his plan to prosper me.

Acknowledgments

"Go home to your friends and tell them how much the Lord has done for you, and how he has had mercy on you" (Mark 5:19 ESV), and "If I alone bear witness about myself, my testimony is not deemed true" (John 5:31 ESV).

I want to acknowledge some important people that have been inspirations in writing my real life story. There have been many people, but I will highlight a few:

I give thanks to my almighty Father God, and his Son, Lord Jesus, for all the love, grace, and mercy given to me and my children and family. Lord, thank you for the oxygen that gave me the chance to write my testimony, for your glory, in this book.

I want to thank my inspirational family. I want to thank my children for staying on board and taking this rough ride of life with me and for their unconditional love. To my children, always remember mommy loves you: hugs and kisses! I want to also thank my two sisters for being my muses, encouraging and supporting me in writing my book and for always looking out for me and my children through the difficult financial and emotional times. I also want to thank my brother for also being my muse, encouraging and supporting me in writing my book, for being my NYPD hero, and for the long intellectual talks in person and on the phone. I thank my parents for raising me, and even after their divorce, they have always remained friends and loving parents to me, my siblings, and the grandchildren. I thank my God-children for their loving hugs and kisses, and I want to also thank my nieces and nephews who have inspired me through their beautiful smiles and love.

Lastly, I want to thank two cousins for they have inspired me through their testimonial love and faith for our Lord Jesus Christ, and almighty Father God.

The Lord inspired me through spoken words of prophecy through two awesome women of God: one from Philadelphia and one from Florida, so I want to thank them. I also want to thank my Pastor from Philadelphia, for bringing forth the Lord's words of truth and light: I was in an emotional prison but the Lord Jesus had already opened the door, but I had to forgive others and myself so that I can step out.

More inspirational people have been the therapists and the PRS personnel that guided me through my recovery from the emotional challenges.

"Be strong and courageous. Do not be frightened and do not be dismayed, for the Lord your God is with you wherever you go" (Joshua 1:9 ESV).

Relationship with God versus The Wall of Idols and Iniquities

THIS CHAPTER WILL OFFER A SNIPPET OF MY explanation about maintaining a relationship with God and his Son, Jesus, and confronting the wall of idols and iniquities that hinder that relationship. I will give you my best explanation about the difference between other beliefs and a Christian's relationship with God and our Lord Jesus.

There are beliefs that have a wall of bricks between God and the believers. The wall resembles all the different idols they have made, kneel to, and worship to as their gods. They are breaking commandments.

> In the Old Testament, it is written "You shall have no other gods before me. You shall not make for yourself an idol in the form of anything in heaven above or on the earth beneath or the waters below. You shall not bow down to them or worship them ..." (Exodus 20:3-5 NIV).

In the New Testament, it is written that Paul "... was greatly distressed to see that the city was full of idols. Paul then stood up in the meeting of the Areopagus and said: "'Men of Athens! I see that in every way you are very religious. For as I walked around and looked carefully at your objects of worship, I even found an altar with this inscription: TO AN UNKNOWN GOD. You are ignorant of the very thing you worship, [so] this is what I am going to proclaim to you. The God who made the world and everything in it is the Lord of heaven and earth and does not live in temples built by hands. For in him we live and move and have our being. Therefore since we are God's off-spring, we should not think that the divine being is like gold or silver or stone – an image made by man's design and skill. In the past, God overlooked such ignorance, but now he commands all people everywhere to repent'" (Acts 17:16, 22-24, 28-30 NIV).

"They knew God, [but] they neither glorified him as God nor gave thanks to him, [and] their thinking became futile and their foolish hearts were darkened. They claimed to be wise, [but] they became fools and exchanged the glory of the immortal God for images made to look like mortal man and birds and animals and reptiles. They exchanged the truth of God for a lie, and worshiped and served created things rather than the Creator -who is forever praised. Amen" (Romans 1:21-23, 25 NIV).

As shown above, in the Old and New Testaments, the Holy Bible speaks to us about idols created by humans, and how the people worshiped these idols instead of the almighty Father God. There are other verses in the Bible that point out how God does not want us to worship idols. Worshiping idols is a sin for which God commands repentance. The wall of bricks resembles sin and causes a separation between God and the people. Sins are also identified as iniquities in the Holy Bible. It is difficult to have a beautiful and close relationship with God when the iniquities become a barrier that separates the people from God. As it reads in Isaiah 59:1-2 (NIV), "Surely the arm of the lord is not too short to save, nor his ear too dull to hear. But your iniquities have separated you from your God; your sins have hidden his face from you so that he will not hear." Likewise, the iniquities become the barrier that separates the people from God's love because "those who cling to worthless idols forfeit the grace that could be theirs" (Jonah 2:8).

Christians are people too. They also had a wall of iniquities in their lives before they chose the Christian belief. Yes, it is impossible to stay without sin and to keep all 613 commandments mentioned in the Holy Bible. God's love for us, his children, saw a problem, so he created a solution. God sent his Son, Jesus, to be crucified for our sins. Note! Every drop of blood Jesus spilled was to cleanse every sin and disease in our lives.

God gives everyone the chance to find the truth. "For God so loved the world, that he gave his only Son, that whoever believes in him shall not perish but have eternal life" (John 3:16 NIV). Recognizing that there is sin in our lives is a huge step toward forgiveness. Then we must accept Jesus Christ as our Lord and Savior by saying the salvation prayer:

> Father God, I believe that Jesus Christ is your son and that he died on the cross for my sins. I am sorry for my sins and the life that I have lived. I "... confess with [my] mouth, [that] 'Jesus is Lord,' and [I] believe in [my] heart that God raised his from the dead, [and I] will be saved" (Romans 10:9 NIV).

Next, find a Christian church to make your home. The continual growth in a relationship with the Lord needs to go through healing. The healing process of our hearts and minds takes place in the church with the feeding of the Holy Word. As we heal, the wall of iniquities starts cracking.

The wall of iniquities will start crumbling. "For our sake he made him to be sin who knew no sin, so that in him we might become the righteousness of God" (2 Corinthians 5:21 ESV). After saying the salvation prayer, we get baptized in water by submersion. We become born-again Christians. "Therefore, if anyone is in Christ, he is a new creation. The old has passed away; behold, the new has come" (2 Corinthians 5:17 ESV).

As we accept our Lord Jesus Christ in our hearts, we will start to feel his love for us and our love for him. However, we need to do our part in maintaining this relationship with the almighty God and his Son, Lord Jesus. We need to keep the bricks from stacking up; we need to continue to fight the battle of sin. And if we slip, we pray to the Lord for strength and forgiveness. We keep our relationship with God and his Son through prayer, reading the Holy Bible, surrounding ourselves with believers of our Lord Jesus for encouragement, and relying on the Holy Spirit's help to up-hold the commandments.

*******NOTE*******

The importance of this chapter is to give all readers the opportunity to accept Jesus Christ in their hearts; in this way, they can have a relationship with God and to recognize the barriers keeping them from him. I believe that after reading the first two chapters, the reader will have a much needed back ground to understand what is read.

I pray that as you read, the Lord will speak to you through my life story. I hope the Lord clarifies the Bible verses knitted in my writing. I pray the Lord shows you how my spiritual weakness had me emotionally unstable and unable to make difficult and safe choices. I pray the Lord highlights that his Holy Word has shed light on many of the problems in my past life. The Lord shows me that he was trying to guide me, but I could not hear his voice. I pray that the Lord takes the blinds off your eyes, the reader, to see and understand your own life.

Jesus says, "I am the way, and the truth, and the life. No one comes to the Father except through me" (John 14:6 NIV).

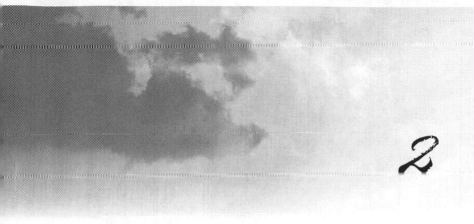

Stepping Back into My Childhood

BEFORE I CONTINUE WITH MY STORY, I NEED TO STEP back to highlight my childhood beliefs, and what is written in God's Holy Word. I see now that my parents' beliefs were not all in agreement with God's Holy Word. In fact, they were breaking God's commandments and establishing these misinterpretations into our family's lives.

I really don't remember them taking me to church unless it was Easter or Good Friday. My parents didn't have a Bible in our home, but God had always been part of our culture. However, my parents also believed that many of Jesus Christ's disciples were saints and that these disciples would answer prayers.

However, God says, "You shall have no other gods before me. You shall not make for yourself a carved image, or any likeness of anything that is in heaven above, or that is in the earth beneath, or that is in the water under the earth" (Exodus 20:3-4 ESV). Yes, the disciples were in the Bible and there were many others in the Bible too. But today we can read and understand that the disciples' purpose was for God and his Son, Jesus, to be glorified. For it is written, "Worthy are you, our Lord and God, to receive glory and honor and power, for you created all things, and by your Will they existed and were created" (Revelation 4:11 ESV).

Unintentionally, my parents cursed our family by not following God's commandments. It is written, "Do not turn aside from any of the commands I give you today, to the right or to the left, following other gods and serving them. However if you do not obey the Lord your God and do not carefully follow all his commands and decrees I am giving you today, all these curses will come upon you and overtake you. The Lord will cause you to be defeated before your enemies. You will come at them from one direction but flee from them in seven ..." (Deuteronomy 28:14-15, 25 NIV). But today, I pray daily for God to forgive my parents and myself for not following God's commandments.

Again unintentionally, my parents also baptized me as a baby. Once I asked them, why I was baptized as a baby? Their response was that it was for my sins to be forgiven, and if I died, I would go to heaven. However, as a baby, what sins did I have? I didn't even know right from wrong. My parents did not know the true meaning of being baptized.

Now, let me clarify the Christian baptism. We believe and accept that there is only one God and his Son, Jesus Christ, and the Holy Spirit. Babies are not baptized because they are too young to have done any sin. Now, when a child grows up to be a teenager, they would have learned right from wrong and that Jesus took all the sins at the cross, and that they can choose to accept Jesus Christ into their hearts and lives and wash away their sins through baptism. As Christians, during the time our babies are growing, we, the parents, need to teach God's Holy Scripture. As parents, we pray that as our children grow, they make the correct choice to get baptized. We choose godparents to help the children follow a Christian love for God and son

Jesus. The parents and the godparents present the babies to God and pray that God directs their hearts and watches over them until they are old enough to choose. At the age of thirteen, the teenagers are older and have choices to make; they can become followers of their peers or distinguish right from wrong and follow God. During the teens' years, the godparents continue to help the parents with the guidance of the teens. They need to intercede with love, understanding, direction, advice, and prayers for God's children. When the teens are old enough, they have a choice to accept our Lord Jesus Christ, son of our almighty Father God, as their Savior into their hearts.

Here is another example, a baby is guided and taught right from wrong by their parents and godparents. As they get older, teens have choices to make; they can become followers of their peers or followers of our Lord Jesus Christ. At this time, when they start making choices for their lives, this is the turning point of accepting God and his Son, Jesus Christ, as their Lord and Savior, and the Holy Spirit. Then they can also make the choice of accepting "... baptism of repentance for the forgiveness of sins" (Mark1:4 NIV). "Whoever believes and is baptized will be saved, but whoever does not believe will be condemned" (Mark 16:16 NIV).

As Christian parents, we will teach God's Holy Word, role model God's love, and give advice with God's blessings and direction to our children, but we cannot force our children or anyone to accept God's Holy Scripture, son Jesus Christ and Holy Spirit. All we can do is pray that our children feel God's love and accept God's love into their hearts by accepting God's son Jesus Christ and getting baptized. For when we "train up a child in the way he should go: even when he is old, he will not depart from it" (Proverbs 22:6 ESV). Yes, we hold the last move! God gave us all the freedom of choice!

Again, I am thankful for my parents and all the beautiful values they taught me: right from wrong as a child, how to be strong, respectful, caring, and loving. However, my parents' home beliefs were confusing, and though I know God was with us always, my parents also had other idols which I know now made God almighty disappointed at us up in heaven. We could not feel God's love because "those who cling to worthless idols forfeit the grace that could be theirs" (Jonah 2:8 NIV). Nevertheless, God is so merciful and gracious to still love us and wait until someone from my generation to recognize our mistake. God gave us the chance to recognize and love only Him, Jesus Christ, and Holy Spirit.

*******NOTE*******

The reason I mention my childhood belief is to show the difference. Likewise, I want to point out that I was not raised knowing the Holy Bible, and so I did not know that I could have a relationship with God, as I do now. But let me emphasize that no matter what my parents' beliefs were, they have been awesome parents, and I will always love them.

3

Choices

TODAY MY "EYES [ARE] OPENED, [AND I CAN] recognize [my lord]" (Luke 24:31 NIV). It has been both the recognizing and connecting with my Lord that has led me to see that God is the perfect author of my life's story. Having a precious love and relationship with my almighty God his son, Jesus, and Holy Spirit has enabled me to see the truth of my life's circumstances through the reading of the Holy Bible. In Matthew 4:4 (NIV), "It is written, 'Man does not live on bread alone, but on every word that comes from the mouth of God.'" Yes! God spoke the words and his perfect manuscript on my life had been written.

But before I can write my story, let me first highlight God's first perfect story. The first perfect story had been written in Genesis 1:27, "God created man in his own image, in the image of God he created him; male and female he created them," and in Genesis 2, I read that the names given were "Adam and Eve." Likewise, I believe that God's manuscript for Adam and Eve was full of the fruits of the spirits: "love, joy, peace, patience, kindness, goodness, faithfulness, gentleness, and self-control" (Galatian5:22-23 NIV). But it was Adam and Eve's disobedience in eating the apple from the forbidden tree that opened the door for iniquity to enter and caused separation from God, and as a result, the iniquities allowed through the door and into my life have been the weakness of my flesh, deception, and the ignorance of God's Holy Word in my heart that has caused me to be misled and make wrong choices in life.

My wrong choices in life have also caused God to work overtime in the editing of his story for me. I pray for forgiveness for my sins and those of my ancestors, parents, and children that have caused God to constantly be editing and directing me back to his first written manuscript of my life. My choices have had God going back to think, erase, and rewrite. Making choices has been the challenges in my life. I know that my choices were not clear because I did not know God. As a lost daughter, I went through many trails. The dark tears in my heart were the pain and trials of my life's experiences. Through all my tears, I would ask, "Why?!" Let me start by asking: Have you ever met a man and said "he is the love of my life!" Me too! Or so I thought.

I recognize now that I was seeking Love! Yes, I had been seeking love, but in all the wrong places. My parents didn't share with me the love I really needed in my early life. I had to first "Love the Lord [my] God with all [my] heart and with all [my] soul and with all [my] mind and with all [my] strength" (Mark 12:30 NIV). I had not met my true love in God because my parents didn't "train [me] in the way [I] should go; [so that] even when [I was old, I would] not depart ..." (Proverbs 22:6 NIV). I did not know "the fear of the Lord is a fountain of life, [that would've] turn [me away] from the snares of death" (Proverbs 14:27 NIV). How could I have known what was really love? I couldn't tell the differences between real love and the snares of death.

My choice of marriage was not based on God's word. I searched for love, my identity, and to be accepted. I thought I would fill the emptiness in my heart by getting married. I searched for love because my parents were too busy with their own marital issues. I searched for myself because as a child I have always had low self-esteem, and I yelled within my heart to be recognized.

I was also trying to adhere to my parents' wishes because I believed it was the decent thing to do. As a young woman, I did not allow myself courting time, and I believed that if I got married, my relationship would last forever. On behalf of my parents and our culture, I do recall my parents telling me that a boyfriend needs to be introduced to the parents for a blessing, and that there should not be any alone time so that the flesh would not overcome. I was young and trying to do the things right. I dated my boyfriend Cain for less than a year, and then we set a date to get married.

I bought a simple white dress at the popular neighborhood clothing store. On the day of my wedding, we went on the train to the City Hall. Yes, the train to City Hall and no special honeymoon get away. After we got married, we went straight to my parents' home because that's where we were going to live. We were renting a small room on the second floor.

Why do couples get married? It is written in Matthew 19: 4-6 (NIV), "At the beginning the Creator 'made them male and female' and says 'For this reason a man will leave his father and mother and be united to his wife, and two will become one flesh. So they are no longer two, but one flesh.' Therefore what God has joined together, let no one separate."

However, nor my husband or I knew the true significance of marriage. God was not within our union. We did not have a true relationship with God. Sadly, we never became "one flesh."

If both of us had known to love the Lord, understand our Lord's ways, and pray on forgiveness for past generation sins, our sins, and keep away from sin, we would have known how to love each other. Only after we have a deep love with God, then will we have been able to learn how to "... love one another, for love comes from God. Everyone who loves has been born of God and knows God" (1 John 4:7 NIV).

*******NOTE*******

Today, I understand that as I searched for answers for the emptiness I felt in my life, I had made wrong choices. God's absences in my heart and life caused me to constantly detour off from God's perfect manuscript for my life. But today, I thank my Father God because he will always love me. "For God so loved the world, that he gave his only Son, that whoever believes in him should not perish but have eternal life" (John 3:16 NIV).

To tie this up, I married in search of love to fill a void in my soul. I really did not know what love was because my parents' beliefs did not instill the true love of God into my early life. God's true love in my heart is what I needed to guide me through my marriage, but my parents did not know that teaching a child about God as a Christian would "train up a child in the way he should go: even when he is old, he will not depart from it" (Proverbs 22:6 ESV). They did not grasp the importance of knowing God as I do today. My marriage and my parents' beliefs did not have a true love relationship with God, Jesus Christ, and the Holy Spirit.

Deception and Evil Resides

LIVING UNDER MY PARENTS' ROOF APPEARED GOOD for a few months. However, waking up under my parents' roof was not what I expected when I got married. Then it started. I was pregnant with my daughter. My emotions started to mess with me. I felt ugly. I was thirsting for attention and love. But instead, my husband gave me less attention which really placed me in the confused state of mind. One thing expecting moms need is attention; they also need beautiful words of recognition, pampering from their husbands, and most of all Love.

During my pregnancy, I questioned my relationship with my husband. I did not feel the connection between us anymore. In all truth, I felt ugly, jealous, angry, and unappreciated. My mom said my feelings were normal because I was pregnant. Nevertheless, my husband did not try hard to show me that I was loved and appreciated.

Here was the problem; neither of us had the real love in our hearts: we were not one. There was a process we had to go through before we would have been able to be united as a couple. First, both of us should have hungered for God's love; our hearts should have felt how much God loves us "For God so loved the world that he gave his one and only Son, that whoever believes in him shall not perish but have eternal life" (John3:16 NIV). Second, we had to "submit [ourselves], then, to God. Resist the devil, and he will flee from [us]" (James 4:7 NIV). Thirdly, after having a relationship with God, we would have been able to "submit to one another out of reverence for Christ. Wives, submit to your husbands, as to the Lord. Husbands love your wives just as Christ loved the church and gave himself up for her. For this reason a man will leave his father and mother and be united to his wife, and the two will become one flesh" (Ephesians 5:21-22, 25, 31 NIV). So neither of us knew how to communicate the love we needed because we really did not have it. Our hearts were not under the spiritual rebirth. As "Jesus declared, 'I tell you the truth, no one can see the kingdom of God unless he is born again'" (John3:3 NIV). We had not been born again; we first needed a deep relationship with God, be reborn, and only then would we have been able to share love or see if it had been God's plan for us to be together.

Now, where was I? Now I remember. My husband did not show me love. My heart filled with pain because I was not feeling loved during my pregnancy. However, becoming a first time mother is a beautiful miracle and love was growing inside of me. A mother's love for her baby is precious. A mother will protect her baby the best way possible. In the Bible, the special love of a mother for her child is written.

In the book of Exodus 1:15-16 (NIV), "the king of Egypt said to the Hebrew midwives ... Shiphrah and Puah. 'When you are helping the Hebrew women during childbirth on the delivery stool, if you see that the baby is a boy kill him; but if it is a girl, let her live.'" In Exodus 2: 1-4 (NIV), a Levite woman "gave birth to a son. When she saw that he was a fine child, she hid him for three months. But when she could hide him no longer, she got a papyrus basket for him and coated it with tar and pitch. Then she placed the child in it and put it among the reeds along the bank of the Nile. His sister stood at a distance to see what would happen to him." But God had already set out a plan, as we read in Exodus 2: 5 (NIV), King Pharaoh's daughter "... saw the basket among the reeds and sent her female slave to get it." Then "Pharaoh's daughter said [without knowledge that it was the baby's sister], 'take this baby and nurse him for me'" (Exodus 2:9 NIV), and she kept him as her son and named him Moses (Exodus 2:10 NIV).

As the Levite woman did what she had to do to protect her son, I would also do anything to protect my baby. About a month after giving birth to my baby girl Liana, my husband Cain got home red eye drunk, and he wanted to carry Liana. I tried to tell him he was not in the right state of mind to carry her. I was scared he would drop her. I placed Liana on the bed. We argued and scuffled. He reached for her, and I blocked him. Without a warning, WHAM! His hand hit me in the face so hard that the strike severely injured my nose. My mother and my brother, David, came into the room, and they took him off of me. Cain left the house ranting on with a slurred speech and with an unbalanced walk.

I could not tune into his slurred speech rampage because I was crying and holding a baby blanket to my painful and bleeding nose. I covered my bleeding nose with a towel. Finally, the bleeding stopped, and I looked at my nose in a mirror. My nose was black and blue and in pain! I really felt that my nose was broken. It wasn't until the next day that I found out the truth about my nose. I went to see the nose doctor. I was sent to take some x-rays of my nose. After the doctor saw the x-rays, he said "let me see what happened." The doctor studied and touched my nose bone, and then a SNAP! My nose was back in place. The doctor said, "There will be swelling around the nose for about a week, but when the swelling comes down, your nose will be ok. Your nose was not broken; it was fractured."

Looking back, I recognize now that the alcohol was an evil that had been residing within our relationship. When my husband was drunk, he was unable to distinguish right from wrong because "wine is a mocker and beer a brawler; whoever is led astray by them is not wise" (Proverbs 20:1 NIV). The Bible explains that he was unable to grasp the reason why he couldn't hold our baby; he was unwise to the consequences.

After a few months, we reconciled, but I asked myself, why. These were the answers in my mind: I reconciled because I blamed myself. I didn't want to become a divorce statistic like my parents. Cain had sobered up and apologized for his actions and words. Either way, we got together again like nothing had happened. The only difference was that every time he raised his hand for something, I would flinch in fear.

*******NOTE*******

Today, I know that evil resided within my marriage back then, but today it has been evicted from my life. I know that God was always with me because without God in my life, fighting evil and deception would have been a lost battle.

Today, I know that to fight deception and evil I have to maintain a true relationship with God. My weapons for war are reading the Bible, listening to worship music, attending and being active in the Lord's temple, and praying daily for a connection and relationship with God, and only then will I be able to resist all deception creeping into my heart, mind, and life.

God Forgives Me

THERE WAS A TIME I WAS VULNERABLE TO THE demands that lead me to do the unspeakable, and then many years later, after being submerged in depression and fear, I became panic-stricken and did the unspeakable by myself.

So here I am, 21 years old, married, still living in my parents' home, and with my eight month old baby girl Liana. I became pregnant again. I told my husband, but his reaction was "How?" He had deliberately caused confusion in me. I immediately became scarred. Then I could hear in his tone; he blamed me for getting pregnant. Then he raised his voice and said, "Kasy, you can't have another baby! Talk to your doctor and tell him that you want an abortion!"

I made the appointment to my doctor's office. Deep down in my heart, I waited for Cain to say, "We're going to keep the baby," but those words were not mentioned. The appointment for the abortion was set. The day arrived, and with tears in my eyes, he took me to the doctor's office. The doctor's office was established on top of a clothing store front. We walked up to the second floor and the doctor lead us upstairs to the third floor. I lay on top of the surgical bed, and the doctor said, "because of your history with asthma, I cannot put you to sleep or give you anything, so you will feel pressure." As I dreadfully lay on the cold surgical table, I wanted to hear Cain say, "Kasy, forget it! Get up and let's get out of here!" But I did not hear any words. Instead I heard my heart yelling as a part of me was ripped out from within me with a suction vacuum tube instrument. I lay my face looking away from Cain as tears poured down my face. Yes, Cain stood there through the whole process. It was finished. I got up, got cleaned up, and dressed myself. We walked out of the surgery room, and Cain didn't show any remorse to what had happened. I had left a part of me! Ignorant and vulnerable, I became a murderer, and he was the husband, instructor, and accomplice. Cain had manipulated and humiliated me. If I had any spiritual free will in me, Cain forced his emotional and spiritual abuse of power over me and I became submissive to his demands. He imposed his non-negotiable decision on my reproductive organs. I could not forgive him, and I could not forgive myself. I cried myself to sleep for months.

Oh wow! Today I write this and my heart yells! Now that I really feel God's love in my heart, I accept that I broke the commandment written in Exodus 20:13 (NIV), "You shall not murder." Why did I allow my husband to have power over my life? Why was I not strong enough to make my own decision? And I'm not going to sit here and place any blames. I know today I had a choice to make. If I had known God, as deep as I do this second, this would not be part of my past today. I know God has forgiven me for that day, and I pray no one reading this judges me. I share this for anyone who is depressed with guilt of doing the same as me. By me telling the world, God is allowing me to judge myself, and by these means, I ask for forgiveness and to clear any cracks in my life that can be targeted by the enemy for deception to creep in. As it is written, "all [of us] have sinned and fall short of the glory of God" (Romans 3:23 NIV), but "if we confess our sins, he is faithful and just to forgive us our sins and to cleanse us from all unrighteousness" (1 John 1:9 ESV). "Let no one despise you for your youth, but set the believers an example in speech, in conduct, in love, in faith, in purity" (1 Timothy 4:12 ESV).

During this time of my life, I felt confused. I could have told him to move out. I had a choice, but I couldn't take a hold of my life; I didn't know what move to take. So we remained together. The physical abuse continued and the mental abuse punctured deep inside my mind and heart.

I drowned in depression. I blamed Cain because he was the first one that instructed me and walked with me to have an abortion. During this time, my voice was invalid. He led me, and he left me in an abyss filled with shock and hollowness. However, years later, I became pregnant again, but in depression and fear, I became anxious about my complications with asthma and not being able to care for another child.

I went to a clinic for the second abortion. Outside the door before I walked in, there were a few people giving out brochures and saying "don't do it!" Father God; I see now those people were your servants! I'm so sorry for my actions! God, I was deaf to your voice and unknowing to your words where you say "whoever welcomes a little child like this in my name, welcomes me" (Mattew18:5 NIV). I walked in and this time I was alone. There were many other young women having abortions. Several women were angry, some were quiet, and others were crying. I was quiet, crying inside, and angry at myself. I was prepared and taken to an operation room. The surgeons didn't want to take the chance of giving me a strong dose of anesthesia to put me into a deep sleep because of my asthma, so I was half asleep and with numbness through all the process. Once again, I felt the suction vacuum tube, but this time I was half-awake; tears of self- hate slid down my face. Shamefully, I had another abortion. Even though I am not blaming him for the second abortion, it was him who pushed me through the door of darkness.

*******NOTE*******

These memories will remain within me forever: The time I was weak to the demand of man, and the time I let fear take a hold of my choices and actions. Both times, I had a choice but I needed strength to stand up for myself. I lacked hope and courage. I lacked free will because I was deeply-rooted in fear and authority to a man from being domestically abused and brittle minded from depression.

At this point, I desperately needed God's true love in my heart. I needed to be reborn as a daughter of God through the acceptance of Jesus Christ. Without God, resisting deception and evil is a lost battle. Therefore, as a born again Christian, I chose to "submit [myself] ... to God; resist the devil, and he will flee from [me]" (James 4:7 NIV). I know now that my heart's bleeding sins have been forgiven because I have confessed my "... sins, [and God] is faithful and just to forgive [my] sins and to cleanse [me] from all unrighteousness" (1 John 1:9 ESV). Thank you God for your merciful words; "there is ... now no condemnation for those who are in Christ Jesus" (Romans 8:1 NIV).

In the name of Jesus, I forgive myself and I pray daily to forgive Cain, too. I cannot walk in the Lord's freedom full of love until I can forgive those that have hurt me including forgiving myself.

6

Black weeds

AFTER LIVING AT MY PARENTS' HOME, WE MOVED to an apartment located on Union Street in Brooklyn. As I sat on my bed at the new apartment, I believed that my life would be better now. In my mind, I gave Cain an excuse for hurting me. Yes, I would tell myself that Cain was abusive because we did not have our own place. As I felt sorry for him for hurting me, a battle in my mind began; I started to replay all the words that he had drilled in my mind. Then I remembered the cliché "sticks and stones may break my bones but words will never hurt me." In my relationship, sticks, stones, and words shattered my heart into a million pieces which left me with no reason to believe that I was worthy of anyone loving me. When Cain was drunk, he would have no regards for my feelings. At first, I tried to say "Stop! No, you're not sober!" His response would be "you're my wife so I'll do what I want!" Time and time again, I felt powerless. I would fear saying "No" because I did not know what to expect. Other times, I would get hit for asking if he could minimize the alcohol.

I even joined him in drinking alcohol a few times because I thought he would love me if I did what he did. However, I got an asthma attack, anxiety, and depression which had my mind resurfacing all the ugly and degrading words he had told me. Drinking alcohol was not who I was! I made a fool of myself because it is written "he who walks with the wise grows wise, but a companion of fools suffer harm" (Proverbs 13:20 NIV). Again, I drank to join his life, but now I understand that his past was filled with pain. He drank to forget and numb his childhood pain, but his pains are not mine to write about.

I was not able to leave because I did not have a true relationship with God. Having God in my life would have stopped the black weeds from growing in my life. My heart was gullible and wide open to death. God says, we can speak life into our lives or death; for "the tongue has the power of life and death ..." (Proverbs 18:21 NIV). I did not have "the full armor of God, so that when the day of evil [came, I] may be able to stand [my] ground" (Ephesians 6:13 NIV) and resist all the deadly words said to me. My heart absorbed all the ugly and degrading words said on to my life: "You're ugly! No one will love you like me! You're a failure! It's your fault! If you leave, you'll come back! You need me!" The black evil seeds grew into black weeds. Yes, my soul had been sleeping and "while [I] was sleeping, [the] enemy came and sowed weeds among [my] wheat" (Matthew 13:25 NIV).

Black weeds are the weeds of fear, depression, low self-esteem, failure, guilt, and loneliness. I feared that I would never find love again and remain alone forever. If I had had a strong relationship with my God and his Son, Jesus Christ, I would have been guided to recognize the pain instead of allowing it to run my life. Likewise, the Lord would have taught me how to self-heal and leave because "God gave [me] a spirit not of fear but of power and love and self-control" (2 Timothy 1:7 ESV). I would not have fallen into depression because the Lord "heals the broken hearted and binds up [my] wounds" (Psalm 147:3 NIV). Low self-esteem would have not settled in my life for I was beautiful because "God created [me] in his image ..." (Genesis 1:27 NIV). God would have told me through the Holy Spirit that I was not a failure because "I can do all things through Him who Strengthens me" (Philippians 4:13 NIV).

*******NOTE*******

As I wrote this piece, I recognized that Low self-esteem and loneliness were the opened doors to replay all my past and even twist it around to blame myself, but all I really have to remember is that "if anyone is in Christ, he is a new creation: the old has gone, the new has come" (2 Corinthians 5:17 NIV).

Today, I recognized that my whole life was filled with black weeds and that the only gardener I needed to destroy all the black weeds was my almighty God.

7

Treacherous Lie

AFTER ABOUT A YEAR OF CONTINUED ABUSE, I HAD found some courage so I filed for divorce. I accompanied a police officer to serve Cain the divorce papers at his job. He did not even open the envelope; instead, he ribbed the envelope in half and threw them towards me.

A few days past. As I sat on the sofa, at the apartment on Union Street, I felt lonely. All of a sudden there was a pound on the door; I was scared so I kept me and Liana quiet. After a few minutes, there was no more pounding at the door. I don't know if it was my fear making me hear things, so with fear and tears, I fell asleep with Liana on the bed.

A month later, because Cain refused to sign the divorce papers, the judge accepted the divorce on the basis of the physical abuse. My marriage was annulled and I was legally divorced. Months of loneliness took me deeper into depression. I got divorced. However, I could not shut these voices of failure, fear, low self-esteem, regret, and Cain's words: "no one will ever love you!" Wow, "the serpent was [a] crafty ... beast ..." (Genesis 3:1 ESV); he had voices dominate my thoughts, made me less responsive to my surroundings, and deaf to God's truth for my life. I felt dead inside.

It is so cruel how a human being can kill another human being with the tongue. It is written in James 3:5-8 (NIV), "Likewise the tongue is a small part of the body, but it makes great boasts. Consider [when] a great forest is set on fire by a small spark. The tongue also is a fire, world of evil among the parts of body, sets the whole course of [one's] life on fire, and is itself set on fire by hell. All kinds of animals, birds, reptiles and creatures of the sea are being tamed and have been tamed by man, but no man can tame the tongue. It is a restless evil, full of deadly poison." I was poisoned, but I did not know it.

I was poisoned by evil words, and the loneliness buried me deep into depression. I would take care of my daughter's needs but then I would place her in her playpen; I did not enjoy her childhood because I was too busy listening to the voices of deception. Weeks of deep depression behind closed doors. The only witness to my depression was Liana, but she could not help me. She was a toddler. She was sad because the only other human to nurture her growth with love was me, but I was lost within my depression to even notice the harm I was doing to her.

Days passed but I could not take this loneliness anymore! I went to Cain's job with an excuse of needing money for pampers. Time and time again, I would go to his job with an excuse; the excuse of pampers turned into a conversation, and I found myself accepting his apologies for hurting me. I did not want to regret not trying, and the voice of failure was too loud in my mind, so we got together again. Being together again this time around, turned out to be positive. He treated me like a princess. He would cook breakfast, lunch, and dinner on the weekends, or sometimes, we would eat out. I was happy I gave our relationship another try. We went shopping together. We did the laundry together. We even played cards together. Yes, I was even feeling guilty of the divorce. I thought that in time we could re-marry, and this time the wedding could be done in a church. I became susceptible to the devil's treacherous lies.

By the fourth month of being together, things started to change. The bottles of beer started showing up in the refrigerator. The days and nights were covered by dark shadows. I went from a princess to a peasant. While living with him, I found myself feeling confused on why things changed in the blink of an eye, but as I write, the Holy Spirit convicts me and says, I had made the mistake of returning with him. I had to "... Resist the devil, and he will flee from [me]" (James 4:7 NIV), but instead, I was living with Cain.

He would arrive late at night covered with alcohol smell. He would try to walk but he would trip. He would curse at whatever was in the way of his unbalanced walks. When I asked, where were you? The slurred responses were unclean to repeat and others were to degrade my abilities as a woman with these words: "I'm a man; you don't tell me what I can do! We're divorced so I don't have to explain myself to you! You're nobody! You're not even a good woman! You're lucky I'm still with you! It's your fault, I'm drinking!" The verbal abuse was constant.

As the abuse continued, my heart was led to protect my daughter Liana. When my daughter would have a little tantrum, Cain would raise his voice at me, and I would quickly pick her up, prepare a bottle of milk, and go to the other room. When Liana drank her bottle of milk, I would rock her to sleep while I, myself, cried, too. Yes, many nights of tears covered my pillow. When I gained a bit of courage, I took out an order of protection.

I asked my dad to change the locks. Then my dad went with a police officer to serve the order of protection at his job.

*******NOTE*******

Today, I understand that my husband had been poisoning me with the tongue, and I also see that I would have never been able to stop him from verbally abusing me. "No man can tame the tongue. It is a restless evil, full of deadly poison" (James 3:8 NIV). Nonetheless, I understand that he needed to choose to seek God to help himself tame the tongue. I understand the verse "submit as a wife," but did God mean to submit till death?

I pray for God to forgive me for neglecting to nurture my daughter with love, and I pray my daughter will forgive me.

Today, I'm a praying warrior for my children, family, and friends. Praying keeps me connected to God "so that [I will] not be outwitted by Satan; for [I will] not [be] ignorant of his designs" (2 Corinthians 2:11 ESV).

8

Devil Prowls

AFTER A FEW DAYS OF CAIN BEING SERVED WITH the order of protection, he was knocking at the door. I kept quiet and ignored it. Then Cain started pounding, and he was able to bust the lock. The door busted open and the alcohol flew in with the wind. With fear in my voice, I said, "you're breaking the court order;" and SLAP! -As I visualize this, I hear "evil people and impostors will go on from bad to worse ..." (2 Timothy 3:13 ESV). - I fell to the floor from the powerful slap which bruised my cheek and injured my nose. I stayed on the floor, and Cain roars, "Did you think a stupid piece of paper was going to tell me what I can't do!" He tore the order of protection into pieces and threw them on me.

I had no means of communication at the apartment, so I waited until I thought he was gone. I placed an ice pack on my cheek. My daughter Liana was crying, so I picked her up from the playpen and went outside to the pay phone. Placing my daughter in front of me and having her little legs hug me towards my back, I wrapped both my arms right under her bottom to hold her up and close to my chest. On my way to the pay phone, I would look all around me in fear that he was following me.

I reached the pay phone. I swung my baby girl over to my left hip, and I held her up with my left arm. With my right hand, I picked up the phone receiver and held it with my left shoulder and left ear. I put in the coins, and with my right hand's pointing finger, I began to push the numbers 9-1- ; then Cain jumped out from behind me with a knife point at my stomach, and he said "Go ahead! Call! By the time the police get here, I will silence you forever!" Envisioning this second in my life, the Holy Spirit says to me that "even Satan disguises himself as an angel of light" (2 Corinthians 11:14 NIV). The smell of alcohol coming from his mouth was as if he had poured a bottle of cologne on himself. I dropped the phone and stood in shock. I froze! I didn't know what to do! I needed help but I was also holding Liana. I pictured myself and my baby girl in severe danger, but my daughter's cry woke me from the shock. Cain had gone. I was confused! Was I dead? I felt my stomach area; did he stab me? I was still standing with my baby girl in my arms. My life flashed in front of me as lightening strikes from the sky. We were still alive because "the whole armor of God ... [stood] against the schemes of the devil" (Ephesians 6:11 ESV).

After crying for a while, I started speed walking to the police station that was four blocks away. I was looking towards my back every second I could. When I finally walked into the police station, I felt relief but scared of what would happen afterwards. I reported all that had happened. The detectives went out to look for him with no luck.

As I mentioned above, I was not spiritually strong enough to keep away or walk away. Cain did not grasp that he had to "be sober-minded; be watchful; [because in our] adversary the devil prowls around like a roaring lion, seeking someone to devour"

(1 Peter 5:8 ESV). Alcohol leads to aggressive words and actions. Many people might say that alcohol tastes good but "in the end it bites like a snake and poisons like a viper. [Our] eyes will see strange sights and [our] minds imagine confusing things" (Proverbs 23:32-33 NIV). Through the alcohol, everything that Cain said, threatened, and acted on was really the devil devouring all of Liana's, and my God given fruits.

*******NOTE*******

As I finished this chapter, tears of thanks slide down my cheeks; I see today that my almighty God had been with me all the time. God protected me! Me and my daughter are alive today because "the whole armor of God, [... stood] against the schemes of the devil" (Ephesians 6:11 ESV).

Protected From Myself

TEARS AND FEAR CREPT UP FROM BEHIND. THE FEAR of trying life on my own with my daughter appeared impossible. The following day, Cain was picked up at his job. I was brought into the police station to identify him and press charges, but my confused heart entangled with emotional lies did not let me. "The heart is deceitful above all things, and beyond cure. Who can understand it" (Jeremiah 17:9 NIV). I could not press charges. I felt sorry for him, and he was the father of my daughter. On the other hand, I was scared that when he was released, he would find me and stab me with repetition. God already had help on the way because "before a word is on my tongue you, [Lord,] know it completely" (Psalm 139:4 NIV). God knew that I couldn't press charges, so God had the detectives take action and process the paperwork with the order of protection that was already in place. The detectives had the report and pictures of the severe black and blue bruises of my face and that is all they needed.

I believe that Cain was arrested so that he could call on to the Lord. For "the Lord hears the needy and does not despise his captive people" (Psalm 69:33 NIV). Cain needed time to weep and pray to recognize his circumstance, choices, and actions. Likewise, I believe that the detectives did not release him because God had placed them there to protect me from myself. Father God "[commanded] his angels concerning [me] to guard [me] in all [my] ways" (Psalm91:11 NIV). I know today that God has a purpose with me for his kingdom. God's love is so huge that he helped me even though I still hadn't accepted his Son, Jesus, into my life. God saw that I was unable to protect myself because I was full of fear, and I lacked the courage to press charges.

Cain was in prison for a few days, and then he was released. He called me to accuse me of pressing charges. I tried to tell him that I didn't press charges, but he did not believe me, and he hung up. I could not sleep nights because Cain did not believe me. Why did I care so much about what he thought? Though my bruises healed in about two weeks, I could not move on with my life. I cried myself to sleep. My heart was not healed. I felt like I was missing something. I felt empty. I loved him, or so I told myself. How could I fear this man and love him, too?

As I write, my Lord answers the above question. My Lord clarifies that "there is no fear in love, but perfect love casts out fear. For fear has to do with punishment, and whoever fears has not been perfected in love" (1 John 4:18 ESV). The perfect love! "... God is Love" (1 John 4:8 NIV). I had to connect to God! In John 14:6 (NIV), "Jesus says, 'I am the way, and the truth, and the life. No one comes to the Father except through me.'" I had to seek Jesus Christ to get connected to my almighty Father God. I had to accept Jesus into my heart and confess all my sins. "Because if [I] confess with [my] mouth that Jesus is Lord and believe in [my] heart that God raised him from the dead, [I] will be saved. For with the heart one believes and is justified;

and with the mouth, one confesses and is saved" (Romans 10:9-10 ESV).

*******NOTE*******

With God's help, I recognize today that the emptiness was a void in my heart. I placed all my heart on Cain thinking he could fill the emptiness. Cain could never really fill me with love when he had his own pain. At this moment, the Lord reveals to me that hurt people are too hurt to show love to others. As we seek to be filled with love, we need to seek God because only he will fill our hearts with love that no human can fill. God "will give [us] a new heart and a new spirit ... he will remove ... [our] heart of stone and give [us] a heart of flesh" (Ezekiel 36:26 NIV). Yes, Father God will show us on how to love him, ourselves, and others. This emptiness in my heart could only be filled with the true love of my Father God, Lord Jesus, and Holy Spirit.

10

Enemies' Trap

WITH FEAR, I MOVED BACK TO MY PARENTS' HOME. Half way into the year, I found myself accepting Cain back in my life. We were back under my parents' roof. Fear was still in my heart, but I felt I needed him by my side to fill the loneliness. Instead of running from Cain, I was going towards him. Depression had moved in and made itself comfortable in my life. Strength and courage had been evicted without my permission. I thought I had a handle of my life. I repeated to myself that I was the cause of the failure in my relationship. This is what I explained to myself time and time again, but this was a lie from the devil! The minute I blamed myself for the beatings, I allowed the enemy access to my heart and emotions.

Instead of blaming myself, what I really needed was my Lord and Savior. I needed to know in my heart that "God gave [me] a spirit not of fear but of power and love and self-control" (2 Timothy 1:7 ESV). I needed to let "my cry come before [my] lord, [to] give me understanding according to [his] word!" (Psalm 119:169 NIV). I should have cried before God to give me strength, courage, forgiveness, and guidance through my next steps and choices. However, my ignorance of my Lord's promise of peace and love led me back into the enemies trap. I accepted Cain back into my life, and I vowed to be a better wife so that he would not have to hit me.

My low self-esteem took away my strength and courage to be free. Blindly and ignorant, my vow positioned me to become submissive with fear. I bought anything needed to care for myself, my daughter and him. I did not ask Cain for money, and if he gave me some money, I would ask, "Are you sure you don't need it?" The response would be "bring me beer," so the master spoke, and I obeyed. On Cain's pay days, he would give me $200 dollars for financial help; afterwards, he would bathe, wear nice clothing, and leave. Hours passed.

As I lay in bed, I look at the clock with scared eyes. "Cling, clang" went the door lock cylinder. "Creek" screeches the warning door as it opens. I close my eyes making believe I'm asleep. I would smell the alcohol entering the room. Then my mind says to get up and offer him food. I got up to ask him, "Are you hungry?" He answered with his deep tone voice, "I don't need your food!" With hidden scared tears in my eyes, at his deep threatening voice, I waited for what was to come. I closed my eyes to go back to sleep, and he grabbed my arm and roared "Don't ignore me!" I responded with fear, "I am sorry; I wasn't ignoring you." Then I would make believe I was going to the bathroom, and afterwards, I would go to sleep on the sofa.

*******NOTE*******

Today, I thank God for blessing me by allowing me to see another day. I was blind and "the enemy pursue[d] me, [and] crush[ed] me to the ground ..." (Psalm 143:3 NIV), but God never abandoned me. Through my blindness and ignorance, my lord whispered in my heart, daughter "Be strong and courageous. Do not fear or be in dread of [him], for it's the Lord your God who goes with you. He will not leave you or forsake you" (Deuteronomy 31:6 ESV).

Today, when I notice that I'm being pursed with sadness and lack of strength, I drop to my knees and let "my cry come before [my] lord, [to] give me understanding according to [his] word!" (Psalm 119:169 NIV).

Prison

MY LIFE WAS A PRISON. THERE WERE MANY PEOPLE that asked me: Why don't you leave him? They would say I was stupid. I remember crying myself to sleep asking myself the same question: "Why can't I leave him?" I know! I know! I had left him many times, and this is why I also cried myself to sleep asking myself: "Why can't I keep away?"

The years with Cain felt like three prison walls with a door made of steel bars, but unlike real prisons, my door was wide open. The only difference from my life prison and a real prison was that the prisoner could not go home, but my prison was my home.

Let me give you some comparisons: A prisoner cannot leave the cell unless the cell bars are opened; I feared stepping a foot out of my home unless it was okay by Cain. A prisoner needs a list of visitors' names a month in advance; I was not even given an option to have visitors because my family was not welcomed. As a means of punishment, a prisoner is placed in the isolation room to cut any communication with others; I was punished publicly. Whenever we went out together, I was not able to greet anyone verbally or with a smile. When I took the chance of stepping out, visiting, or greeting anyone, Cain would verbally or physically correct me when I got home.

I see now that not only was my flesh imprisoned but my soul was drowning and imprisoned. Let me break down, "imprisoned." I had allowed the clean and beautiful soul God had given me to be imprisoned. I had given the devil the ability to instill deception: depression, fear, failure, low self-esteem, lack of strength, lack of confidence, and false love into my soul. Let me explain, God gave me a "child's heart," but when I allowed the devil's deceptions into my heart, my "child's heart" was covered with a black blanket. The black blanket blinded my beautiful heart and making it difficult to see that the doors to my prison were wide open. On top of blindness, I also feared taking any steps out of my prison physically and spiritually. I "imprisoned" my body and soul.

I will repeat. I allowed my body and soul to be imprisoned. No matter how many times I would leave, I would come back to my prison because my body and soul were not free. To free myself, I had to first fight the deceptions, so I would have been able to take that first step out of the prison door. I needed to fight "fear." I needed to trust God in that everything would be okay so that I could leave and stay away, but I needed both my body and soul to take the step together. I had a choice to Fear Cain or Trust God?

******NOTE*******

As I write, the Lord reveals that I did not really know God like I do today, and for such reason, I remained with a man that fed me degrading words and actions. Today, I thank God for he has allowed me to see the big screen play of my past life, and he has let me understand and learn from my past choices.

Jesus Christ paid the price for all my sins, so my imprisoned body and soul always had the opportunity to leave the prison. After the salvation prayer and accepting Jesus Christ as my Lord and Savior, Jesus handed me the authority for my body and soul to step out of prison! "... The Lord set prisoners free" (Psalm 146:7 NIV).

Today, I remind myself that to be free my body and soul have to be focused on my Lord. When things get tough, and I feel that I am going to imprison myself, I say: "... the Lord set prisoners free" (Psalm 146:7 NIV). If fear is sneaking up, I say: "When I am afraid, I will [place my] trust in you [Lord]" (Psalm 56:3 NIV).

12

A Glimpse of Hope

AS I MENTIONED PREVIOUSLY, I THOUGHT IF I worked more and brought more income, Cain would be happier and love me more but this was a lie from the devil. However, I also told myself that if I had a career, I would not need to stay by his side because I would become financially stable. As a result, I decided that I needed to pursue a college bachelor's degree. I registered and completed the admissions process to attend a City University of New York, and I took up Elementary Education.

Because I still lived under my parents' roof, the CUNY I attended was a few train stops away. On my first day of college, I truly felt that my whole life was going to change for the better. My actions to seek a college degree made me feel good about myself and that I would be able to become financially independent. My first semester consisted of remedial courses. The remedial courses consisted of high school reviews in math, reading, and writing, and then assessments in these areas. The goal was to pass all assessments, and then I would be able to register into the regular college courses needed to reach my degree. I had the opportunity to earn some money through college work study at $5.00 an hour. This money helped me with the purchase of books and supplies for college. My courses were paid through Pell Grant, but the truth is I still had to give up some of my needs to cover other expenses.

The day I started college, I felt courageous and happy. I felt like someone important because I was surrounded by other students that wanted to learn and be successful. God's hand was involved in my pursuing an education. Though I had not yet prayed the salvation prayer, I believe that God was editing his first story for my life. God saw the mess I was in, so God did what he does best. In Psalm 32:8 (NIV), God says "I will instruct you and teach you in the way you should go; I will counsel and watch over you." God took me in the path of an Education.

While I was on campus following my courses, I felt happy like if I had been someone else. As you might have noticed, I registered for college against Cain's approval. When I headed home after classes, I felt different. My life got difficult at home. Let's recap a piece of my life, remember I was not allowed to mingle with anyone because I would face the consequences at home. Though my life felt like a prison, I know God was guiding me step by step when I took the bold move of attending college. I can hear God speaking to me now: "'for I know the plans I have for you,' declares the Lord, 'plans to prosper you and not to harm you, [and] plans to give you hope and a future'"(Jeremiah 29:11 NIV).

Once again I had this spark of courage; I separated myself from Cain. This was not easy for me. When he finally left, the enemy's deceptions burst out. I felt lonely, and I repeated to myself that I was a failure in my relationship. I felt guilty in sending my daughter's father away. Our relationship was like a roller coaster ride; we would separate and get back together again. I was confused because of all the deceptions in my life.

I began to experience the life of a single mom. Attending CUNY gave me the hope that I was somebody, but there was a struggle in my inner thoughts. I felt lonely because I still had not invited my Lord and Savior into my heart and soul.

During my first two years working towards my CUNY degree, my battles were ongoing. My fooled heart was missing Cain. My finances were also tight because I was not earning much in college work study, and I struggled in deciding on how to spend the little I had. Do I buy clothes for my daughter or buy school supplies? While I tried to be strong to remain a single mom, there was a simultaneous battle of deception that I was the cause of the failure in my relationship. As a result, I allowed my relationship to rekindle time and time again. When things got abusive, I would break it off. I had a heart full of discouragement, deception, and depression. I feared being alone, and I did not want to be a failure in my relationship.

*******NOTE*******

God has always been with me, but I was blind and could not see, recognize, or feel God's movement in my life. Today, I thank God for "instructing [me] and teaching [me] in the way [I] should go" (Psalm 32:8 NIV) towards a career. God was preparing me for my future; he knew my ignorance and the emptiness in my heart because I had not yet met my Lord Jesus to be truly connected to my almighty Father God's true love.

13

Tears on My Pillow

ONE YEAR INTO COLLEGE, I FELL FOR CAIN'S deception and I became pregnant. Was I back with Cain? No, I did not go back to live with him, but he would come around to visit me and Liana at my parents' home. Unfortunately, I had to put my college education goal on hold.

During this pregnancy, God had helped me overcome some of my low self-esteem. I felt beautiful. I went to the hair salon to have my hair cut and styled to hang on my shoulders. I really loved how the clothes looked on me as I dressed up. I felt that I had more energy. Cain's description of displaying love was by visiting our daughter, our unborn baby, and hurt me with confusing words of love. With a teasing voice, he said, "How is my belly?" Sometimes, he would suit up like going to a party and bring me flowers. My eyes would believe that he was looking handsome for me. My heart started beating, but "the heart is deceitful above all things ..." (Jeremiah 17:9 NIV). My mind would pound me with guilt: I'm at fault! I pushed him out! I'm to blame!

Once a week, I was visited by Cain. He did not smell like alcohol. His visits confused me. Did he really stop drinking?

Did he really love me or not? Was it my pride keeping us apart? My mind had a battle going on because when he visited, he would be so kind and have words of love for me; then he would leave! I was "... tempted when [I was] lured and enticed by [my] own desire" (James 1:14 ESV). I would not hear from him until the next visit. Months passed by, and during the nights, I would cry myself to sleep. Tears landed on my pillow with an ongoing battle in my mind.

It was time! A baby was coming into this world of confusion. When there are miracles of birth, we have to accept that God is real! I thank God for allowing me the miracle of a baby once more. I held my baby boy in my arms, and then Cain arrived in the room. He stood there as if all was fine. At least, we were able to discuss a name. We gave him the name Tony. Because Cain and I were no longer married, the dad's last name had to be forwarded by filling out the paternal recognition form. I felt happy because I was a new mom but I was also emotionally unstable. Now that I had two children, I felt I had to give our family another chance.

We tried to unite our family again. Cain would visit his children and me every week at my parents' home. After about ten months, we moved to a small two bedroom apartment by the "J" train. I remember that it was about ten months because Tony was standing up in his crib by holding on the crib's railings. I was a stay at home mom, and Cain was working to bring in the income.

After we had moved into the apartment, the dark shadows of evil started showing its presences in my home. Alcohol re-entered in my home, but I tried to handle it different this time. Instead of getting upset because of the alcohol, I tried to accept his addiction of alcohol and life choices. I tried to learn to accept Cain's going out to be with friends. As soon as he walked in after work, I prepared his nice clothes for that evening. As Cain took a shower, I ironed his clothes and got them ready for him to go hang out by himself. I did this many weekends. After too many weekends of being home alone, I would beat myself with tears and words that I was not worthy enough to go out with him. Cain was embarrassed to walk with me by his side.

Once again, my nights were lonely with my two children because their father would go spend the nights drinking, and then he would come back home drunk and angry. I believe if I had kept my mouth shut, things would not have escalated. I guess I instigated by asking, Why do you drink? Don't you see what the alcohol is doing to you and our family? Cain responded by verbally degrading me, physical abuse, and walking out.

One evening, Cain came from work drunk; I served him homemade spaghettis and meatballs. I asked him, "can I get some money to buy pampers," and in a flash, Cain got up and threw the plate of spaghettis at me, but he missed and it slammed against the wall! Then he walked out. I started crying. My daughter was 4 years old, and she knew when I was sad. When Liana's 1 year old baby brother Tony started crying, she would say to me, "Don't worry mom; I'll take care of Tony." Liana took Tony a bottle of milk. After a while, I went into the room, and Liana and Tony were fast asleep. I walked out and went to the medicine cabinet. It hurt! I wanted a happy family and I felt empty! I took an unopened bottle of Nyquil and drank it all up. I did not want to ever wake up. However, I felt sleepy, on and off, for about three days, but thank God I was at least able to care for my children though I was in a daze.

*******NOTE*******

Today, I recognize that suicide should never be taken as an escape from an emotional battle; God says, "Do not be over wicked and do not be a fool- why die before your time" (Ecclesiastes 7:17 NIV). I am living evidence in so many ways of God's grace. Though I attempted to commit suicide more than once, God kept me alive.

Today, I know that I should not allow myself to drown in emotional pain; instead, I have and I will continue to seek the help I need through prayer and mental health therapy. I know some might not agree with me in all. The misconception that mental health therapy is for crazy people leads many to remain in the realm of depression and confusion. In search of my identity, God has guided me to see my image in him. I believe that God has also guided me to seek mental health therapy for me to learn on how to cope with life's changes; how to stay alive.

Yes, seeking our identity will help us with how we view ourselves. There are many people going through low self-esteem and more. Many people's confusion and emotional pain emerge from the past and not knowing their identity. They are foreign on how much they are really worth and loved by God!

14

Oxygen

LIVING IN THE APARTMENT BY THE "J" TRAIN DID not last long. Though I had my two children, loneliness became my friend, so I moved back to my parents' home. I struggled to keep myself afloat financially, emotionally, and courageously. I forced myself to go back to college. I took up working in the admissions office for extra funds to buy my text books and any other educational needs. I was doing okay, or so I thought. Going to college became my escape from reality. I buried my depression in a mountain of class assignments. My character around my classmates and professors was full of smiles, but my heart's true pain poured out as soon as I shut my home door behind me.

The month was January 1994, and it was a day like any other day. A new semester was beginning, so I was assigned to the admissions table. The severe cold weather set my asthma in motion, but instead of seeking medical attention, I tried to heal myself by using the nebulizer at home. By the third day of having limited air flow, I do not know how I even made it to and from the college. As I sat at home, with the nebulizer mouth piece in my mouth; my lungs were tirelessly pushing oxygen

55

through my air ways, but it was a losing battle. With limited oxygen, I asked my dad to take me to the hospital.

Gasping for oxygen, I forced myself to walk into the emergency room; the registration window appeared miles away, and my tears full of oxygen escaped my lungs without me able to restrain them. As I tried to inhale oxygen by opening my mouth for air to go through my windpipe, I felt that the tube connecting my windpipe and my lungs were blocked by rocks. Some air must have sifted between the openings in the rocks because I reached the window and the word "asthma" slipped out. I was wheeled in. An oxygen mask was placed on me, and I was given an injection of epinephrine. Then I was given a second injection of epinephrine. The doctor came back to listen to my lungs' airway, and I was feeling a little better. Then the nurse comes in with another injection of epinephrine, and in the blink of an eye, I felt my windpipe clogging up as like with cement. My oxygen stopped! My eyes opened wide trying to yell but no words or sound came out of my mouth. I saw the doctors and nurses running towards me with a hand held pump mask. As I struggled for oxygen, I did not expect a mask getting closer to my face. The thought that flashed in my mind was that the mask was going to kill me, so as I battled for oxygen and limited strength, I tried to push the nurses and doctors away, and LIGHTS OUT!

I went into a coma. I felt as light as a feather. Then I was in the air. I could not understand what was happening; next, I flew towards some soft grey clouds. Then I looked down and saw ME! My body was going through a CT-Scan radiology machine. As I continued to go through the clouds, I was inside a room where church pews were against the walls. As I was softly placed on a floor of clouds, I moved forward and felt a presence of someone by my side. As I heard a voice speaking to me, I also saw a hand extend to give me a comforter. I was told to take the comforter and find a spot under the pews. I searched under every pew, but there was no space for me. Each pew was occupied by people and their comforters. I could not find a spot! What did this mean?! Then the voice said it was my choice to stay or go through the door that appeared in front of me; I opened the door, and I was walking on light bluish clouds. As I moved on through and over the clouds, I saw a white cross connected to a long pole on a triangle roof top.

Immediately, I heard a television say "a day till Valentines. Have you bought your loved one's gift?" I heard the voice of my aunt and my grandpa, but how could that be? I thought to myself, I live in New York and they live in Puerto Rico. My vision was blurred; I tried to clear it. I saw white and when it finally cleared up, I saw my aunt wearing a white coat and my grandpa standing near her. I couldn't speak because I was on a ventilator – process of inserting tubes down my throat for a machine to breath for me. Thoughts raced in my mind: What happen?! Why is my family from Puerto Rico here! Where is here?! Then I recognized I was in a hospital room. I felt a tube through my mouth and down my windpipe, and I felt another tube under my left arm and in through the left side of my lung. Then I heard someone say, "Thank you God!"

Doctors surrounded me. As they checked all the machines surrounding me, they easily pulled out the tubes in my throat. They told me to try to swallow, so I did. Then one doctor asked me, "What day is it, today? Can you speak?" I swallowed again and forced myself to respond. In a strenuous voice, I responded in a question, "January 29?" To my shock, the answer was February 13th.

A few days after, I learned that I had gone into a coma and that the doctors had told my parents to consider pulling the plugs on the life support because they said the machines were breathing for me and that I was gone. At this second, Jesus must have said to my parents, "... the girl is not dead but asleep" (Matthew 9:24 NIV) because my parents asked the doctors for one more day. All it took was one night for God to do a miracle. As it is written in John 14:11 (NIV), "Believe me when I say that I am in the Father and the Father is in me; or at least believe on the evidence of the miracles themselves," and today my parents and family say, God brought me back.

Now, I did not get up and started walking like Lazarus in John 11:43(NIV), or like the invalid man by the healing pool John 5: 5-9 (NIV), but to inhale and exhale oxygen on my own without a machine was the miracle I needed to live. God's solution to this piece of my life was oxygen!

My body muscles lost all strength. I could not pick up my head because my neck was like a newborn's neck. I could not pick up my arms. I could not walk; my feet were diagnosed by doctors as dropped feet because I had no strength in my ankles to hold my feet up in an "L" shape. My left lung had collapsed. My life will go on with my right lung being the stronger lung.

As I was propped up to reach the food tray table, the tears rained down my face because I could not lift up my arms to the table. I remember, saying God "please help me," and a nurse would walk in to feed me. The nurses changed my bed by rolling my body on to a hammock like crane. A physical therapist came to my room to help me lift my neck, arms, hands, and legs. I regained the strength to sit up on the bed. I was taken to physical therapy everyday so I could strengthen all the muscles I had lost during the 15 days in coma. Every night, I prayed by giving thanks to God for the oxygen and for regaining my strength. Before I was discharged, I had regained at least 50% of my muscle strength.

*********NOTE*********

Today I am grateful for God gave me life after being in a coma and redirected my path from being placed in the ice box. I know that what had happened to me was big, but as stated in 1 Peter 5:10 (NIV), I know God "... himself restore[d]" and [made] me "strong, firm, and steadfast" because God gave me oxygen and he renewed my strength.

God's Waiting Room

I HAVE TAKEN EXCERPTS FROM MY PREVIOUS chapter to go in depth to highlight God's Holy Word in connection to the grace I received. There is a waiting room.

Lights out! Oxygen terminated! I felt as light as a feather. I was in the mists of soft grey clouds and looking down at me! My body was going through a CT-Scan radiology machine. As I read in Psalm 91:4 (NIV), I understand now that the Lord covered me "with his feathers, and under his wings [is where I found] refuge; his faithfulness [was my] shield and rampart."

My Lord was in control of my destination. I was "... in the clouds [with] the Lord in the air" (1 Thessalonians 4:17 NIV) and taken into one of God's rooms. Yes, a room! Why not a room? My almighty Father God's house has many rooms. As the Lord Jesus says, "My Father's house [has] many rooms; if it were not so, I would have told you. I am going there to prepare a place for you" (John 14:2 NIV).

As I was taken through the clouds, I was lightly placed on a cloud. As I moved forward on the clouds, unsure of where I was, I looked at my surroundings. I was in a room that had church pews that were against the walls and extended from corners to corners. As I continued to move forward on the clouds, I felt a beautiful and peaceful presence of someone right beside me.

The presence I felt was my Lord! He says, "My presence will go with you, and I will give you rest" (Exodus 33:14 NIV). I could hear a voice speaking to me, and simultaneously, I saw a hand extending out in front of me and holding a comforter. The Lord's voice said: "take the comforter and find a spot under the pews." I searched under every pew, but there was no space for me. Each pew was occupied by people and their comforters. I could not find a spot! What did this mean? I know the Lord was letting me know that he will "... comfort [me] in all [my] troubles ..." (2 Corinthians 1:4 NIV). The Lord's voice said, "It's your choice to stay or go through the door." I was going to ask, "What door?" Then in the blink of an eye a door appeared in front of me to my right. God's love and grace had shown me the door to my return.

In the time of my soul's despair, the Lord guided my soul back towards my body and with that giving me and my family hope. My "Lord is my shepherd; I shall not be in want. He makes me lie down in green pastures. He leads me beside quiet waters. He restores my soul. He guides me in paths of righteousness for his name's sake. Even though I walk through the valley of the shadow of death, I fear no evil for [the Lord is] with me; [his] rod and [his] staff, they comfort me" (Psalm 23:4 NIV). In 2 Corinthians 1:6-7 (NIV), "... if we are comforted, it is for [our] comfort, which produces in [us] patient endurances of the same sufferings we suffer. And our hope for [the Lord] is firm because we know that just as [he] shares in our sufferings, so also [he] shares in our comfort."

Yes, my Lord comforted my soul on the journey to God's waiting room. My Lord comforted me with his presence as he handed me a comforter. A comforter to help me feel less worried; Jesus asked "the Father and he [gave me] another counselor, to be with [me] forever the Spirit of truth" (John 14:16-17 NIV); "Now the Lord is the Spirit, and where the Spirit of the Lord is, there is freedom" (2 Corinthians3:17 NIV). My Lord handed me the Holy Spirit! The Spirit of Truth! "When he, the Spirit of truth comes, he will guide [me] into the truth" (John 16:13 NIV). My Lord's voice guided me to make a choice. I could stay in the waiting room alongside all the others or I could choose the door. As I held the comforter, I was able to listen and be guided towards the truth of freedom. I chose the door. Yes! The Spirit of Freedom!

*******NOTE*******

Today, I understand why my Lord handed me the comforter. The comforter was the Holy Spirit which guided my soul towards the truth and freedom; most of all, my Lord gave me the comforter to comfort others! Because I had seen and felt God's love, mercy, and grace, in God's waiting room in heaven, I am now led to comfort others with my testimony. "Praise be the God and Father of our Lord Jesus Christ, the Father of compassion and the God of all comfort, who comforts us in all our troubles, so that we can comfort those in trouble with the comfort we ourselves have received from God" (2 Corinthians 1:3-4 NIV).

16

White Cross

AT MY DISCHARGE FROM THE HOSPITAL, I NEEDED help to walk to the car. I was walking the steps of a toddler. On the drive home to my parents' house, my heart was pouring thoughts of deception that raced through my mind: I must have deserved what happen to me. I am never going to walk like I use to. I'm a failure, so I gave up.

Weeks passed, and I regained some strength, so I started trashing all of my college graded assignments. I repeated to myself: if I go back to college, something else will happen, so why bother. I accepted Cain back in my life because I was told he was crying, when doctors advised to pull me off of life support. I believed he really loved me, I became a stay at home mom. I was unable to continue college or take a job because I was still weak, so I applied for Social Security Income, but I was denied. This did not surprise me because in my eyes, I was a failure.

I continued living with a man that apparently had not changed. His addiction to alcohol was stronger than the tears he had shed when I was in the hospital. He criticized my every effort. His words poisoned my soul. As I now understand, words can speak life or death. In Romans 3:13 (NIV), "[the] throat is an open grave; [people use] their tongues to practice deceit. The poison of vipers is on their lips." I repeat! His words poisoned my soul! He crocheted degrading words into my mind and heart. My life reached a point that being physically hurt was better than the words that hurt me like pins and needles! My physical and mental abusive relationship became part of my life style. Being happy, was not a requirement for me to live. I was content with my unhappy life. I was able to function. My emotions were locked away and were not allowed to peek out. I had to be a good mom because that is all that mattered, but I also tried to be a good wife. As I tried to sleep at nights, I would cry and blame myself for the tears.

I functioned because my emotions were imprisoned and surrounded with dark shadows of deception. However, the prison door was never shut. The prison door was wide open! The Lord Jesus was waiting for me to step out of prison, so he can help me heal emotionally.

During this time, my cousin Monica was talking to me about God, Jesus, and Holy Spirit. She would tell me how Jesus our Lord and Savior paid for all our sins and that I was invited to her church. She explained God's enormous love because he sent his Son, Jesus Christ, but I ignored her words. I could not picture myself being loved. Yes, the enemy was working overtime! The enemy would have me saying to myself, you need to stay home; if you go to church, things will get bad for you. "As for the scoundrel – his devices are evil; he plans wicked schemes to ruin the poor with lying words" (Isaiah 32:7 ESV). I was battling with my cousin's invitation for weeks.

Finally, I accepted Monica's invitation to her Christian Church. I took my first step. I accepted Jesus Christ, as my Lord and Savior. I became a Christian. I started to go to church with the kids. I made sure to leave the house before Cain arrived from work because I was going without his permission. When I would leave the church, I felt so energized and courageous that I did not care about the consequences that waited for me at home. I felt joy, but when I reached home, placed my right hand on the door knob, turned it, and pushed in to open, the joy I felt was instantly replaced with fear. Most of the time, Cain would be sleeping, but this day he was awake. He looked at me when I walked in. I refused to look towards his direction, but I knew ignoring him was going to cost me. I told the kids to go get ready for bed, and as I felt my heart beat, I looked towards his way. I waited for the degrading words, but he said he was leaving. He packed his suitcase and left.

I continued going to church. I felt joy and laughter in my life; I felt strange because I did not remember the last time I laughed. I know now that "a joyful heart is good medicine, but a crushed spirit dries up the bones" (Proverbs 17:22 ESV). After a few months of attending the church, I was ready to be baptized. On July 1995, I was baptized; my sins were washed away, and I was forgiven in the name of Jesus Christ. I became a re-born child of God. I became very hungry for God's love and the Holy Word. For "it is written; 'Man shall not live by bread alone but by every word that comes from the mouth of God'" (Matthew 4:4 ESV). I went every Sunday to Bible Study to learn something new every day. In addition, I registered to a private Bible School Institute to go deeper into studying the Holy Word.

After a year of studies, there was a graduation ceremony. The graduation was taking place at an affiliated church. As I was driving towards the reserved church, I couldn't believe my eyes. As I followed the Pastor's church van, I glanced at the church as we pulled into the block. The church was beautiful. All of a sudden, my vision was glued onto the top of the church.

My jaw hanged opened. I was in shock! My eyes visualized my outer body experience while I was in coma. I saw a white cross connected to a long pole on the triangle roof top. In fact, my eyes were so connected to the white cross on the roof top that the Holy Spirit had to yell "Watch it!" Immediately, I switched my eyes off the white cross to look at the church van in front of me, and I stepped on the break!" God had given me a vision of his purpose for me. This was that VISION! Why now? "For still the vision awaits its appointed time: it hastens to the end; it will not lie. If it seems slow, wait for it; it will surely come; it will not delay" (Habakkuk 2:3 ESV).

I almost had a car accident! That was just too close! As I regained my focus, I parked and stepped out starring at the white cross. God took me back to when I was in a coma where the machines were breathing for my lungs, but God gave me a choice to return. His manuscript on me had more. It is written in Jeremiah 29:11 (ESV), "For I know the plans I have for you, declares the Lord, plans for welfare and not for evil, to give you a future and hope." I saw the exact white cross connected to the long pole on top of the triangle roof. Yes, God had shown me a piece of my future. During the Bible institute graduation ceremony, I tried to grasp what I had just seen!

God's story with my life was not done, and this is why I was given the choice to walk through the door.

*******NOTE*******

Today, I see that the white cross confirmed that God had led me in the direction of his purpose for my life. Though I was not yet totally healed, some cracks had been created for my emotions to peek out and see the light. As I feed my heart with the Holy Word today, I feel the light that shines as I walk in God's word. "For at one time [there was] darkness, but now [I am] light in the Lord. [I] walk as [a child] of light" (Ephesians 5:8 ESV). God's word "is a lamp to my feet and a light to my path" (Psalm 119:105 ESV).

Lifestyle Does Not Fill My Heart

I CONTINUED GOING TO CHURCH WITH MY COUSIN. Yes, my children's dad left us because I was not abiding to his demands of isolation, and he could not control me as he saw fit for I lived at my parents' home. The courage came from my Lord's love. It is written, "Be strong and courageous. Do not be afraid or terrified because of [him], for the Lord your God goes with you. He will not leave you nor forsake you" (Deuteronomy 31:6 NIV).

As I continued to go to church, I saw blessings. After a year of God's mercy where he allowed me to wake from the coma and to regain my strength, I decided to return to College. While I lived at my parents' home, I placed applications for an apartment at the projects. I prayed for God's blessing over my children and myself to have our own place. In less than a year of having placed the application for an apartment, I received the response for public housing in Queens, New York; I was approved a two bedroom apartment on a 10th floor.

As I lived in my new apartment with my children, all was good but with some challenges. At first, my daughter would be picked up by the neighborhood school bus. However, she was getting bullied, so with a lot of paper work, I transferred her back to her childhood school in Brooklyn. The next challenge was the elevator conditions.

Every morning, I got my children ready for school: brush their teeth, made breakfast, and clothed them. As I stepped out the door, I was cautious of my surroundings. Then as we walked to the elevator, I wondered daily if the elevator was working, and if we could resist the urine stench, and if we were taking the stairs from and to the tenth floor. Yes, the elevator was a sweet and sour necessity. Walking out the building, I was blessed to have a car. I put my children into the car and buckle both of their seatbelts. Then I got in the car, buckled up, and we drove off.

Next, I drive my daughter to Brooklyn and drop her off at her school. Then I take Tony with me to college. I park the car in the student parking lot. Then I take Tony, our backpacks, and walked towards the college. First, I drop Tony off at the Pre-K affiliated with the university, and afterwards, I run to my class. In between classes, I earned a little money through college work-study. At the end of my classes, I crossed the street from my college towards the Pre-k school to pick up Tony. Then I drove off to pick-up Liana at my mom's (whom had already picked her up from school); finally, we all drove back home to our apartment in Queens.

There were days I had to add stops to my already busy day like going food shopping, doctor's appointments, or washing clothes at the laundry mat that couldn't wait for the weekend. I also attended church Tuesday, Thursday, Saturday evenings, and Sunday mornings. Helping my daughter with her homework was another priority. I also made sure my children were bathed, feed, and placed to sleep. Lastly, I had to budget, write checks for the bills, complete my college assignments, and maybe sleep. Wow, was I superwoman? No! I recognize today I am the daughter of the almighty God. I see now the truth is "I can do all things through him who strengthens me" (Philippians 4:13 ESV).

My income was not over flowing, but I was blessed. I worked at the university because of the college work study, and the Pell Grants paid the tuition, and I was approved a student loan for my last semester. God blessed me with some financial resources for rent and food, and I also had a credit card. I did not depend on child support, but when anything came through, it was a blessing. I was surviving with my income, but God did not allow my income struggles to break me. It is written in 1 Corinthians 10:13 (NIV), "... God is faithful; he will not let you be tempted beyond what you can bear. But when you are tempted, he will also provide a way out so that you can stand ..." and endure it.

All was good. Day after day, I repeated my schedule. I felt good! I was going to college, and I cared for my children. I had family love and unity. I had an apartment, a car, and I went to church. However, I was not happy. I felt lonely and I still did not feel beautiful. I was lacking something. My heart was empty. "A glad heart makes a cheerful face, but by sorrow of heart the spirit is crushed" (Proverbs 15:13 ESV). My heart had not yet been filled completely with my Lord's love. I still felt anxious and worried. I lacked a relationship with my Lord Jesus. It is written:

> "Therefore, I tell you, do not be worry about your life, what you will eat or what you will drink, or about your body, what you will wear. Is not life more than food and the body more than clothes? Look at the birds of the air: they do not sow or reap or store away in barns, and yet your heavenly Father feeds them. Are you not of more value than they?

Who of you by worrying can add a single hour to his life? And why do you worry about clothes? See how the lilies of the field grow; they do not labor or spin. Yet, I tell you that not even Solomon, in all his, splendor was dressed like one of these. If that is how God clothes the grass of the field, which is here today and tomorrow is thrown into the fire, will he not much more clothe you. O, you of little faith? So do not worry, saying, 'What shall we eat?' or 'What shall we drink?' or 'What shall we wear?' For the pagans run after all these things, and your heavenly Father knows that you need them. But seek first his kingdom and his righteousness, and all these things will be given to you as well. Therefore do not worry about tomorrow, for tomorrow will worry about itself. Each day has enough trouble" (Matthew 6: 25-34 NIV).

Though the pieces of my life were fitting together, I still felt anxious and worried because I lacked a true relationship with my Lord Jesus.

*******NOTE*******

Today, I recognize that my anxiety came from the inability to place my Lord first in my daily life. I see that God blessed my dad financially, and in turn my dad paid my car insurance and any car expense as I attended CUNY. God had friends, professors, and supervisors at the university bless me with lunch. God placed my children in my life to keep my heart alive and to overcome. God gave me a loving mom, dad, two sisters, and my brother. God also gave me children, nieces and nephews to bless me in many ways because the main blessings are family love and unity.

Today, I want to take this moment to thank God first and utmost for his awesome love and for answering my prayers. God has blessed me with family love and unity. He blessed me with the spark of courage to step out on faith to pursue a bachelor of arts. God showed me where to go listen to his Holy Word. God blessed me with his Son, Jesus Christ, who washed away my sins. Jesus Christ gave me the choice to be a new creation with hope and faith because every morning was a new day with more blessings. For it is written, "Therefore, if anyone is in Christ, he is a new creation. The old has passed away: behold the new has come" (2 Corinthians 5:17 ESV). I have concluded that I could have been the riches person on earth, but it has been my Lord Jesus, and his Holy Word in my life that has me writing today what God has birthed in my heart.

18

Power of the Tongue

AS I CONTINUED LIVING IN THE PROJECTS, I KEPT myself strong as I cared for my children. I continued my studies and going to church. My daily schedule filled my days, so I was too busy to feel lonely. There were times that I questioned myself on how many days I went to church. In fact, there were many days that I felt exhausted. I started doubting the need of the many times I attended church, but I did not want to lose hope.

I would force myself to go to church at least two days out of four. The travel time from Queens to the church in Brooklyn was about 30 minutes or 50 minutes with traffic. Going to church gave me comfort, a feeling of peace, and I felt alive. Yes! I felt alive.

Before I took my cousin's invitation to church, my body was walking but I was humanly dead. I would flinch at anyone's hand gesture. I felt worthless and I would cry to Cain's deep voice. I would walk with my neck slouched and eyes looking at the floor. I avoided a mirror, and I feared speaking to anyone. I did not want to exist. I was really depressed. The invitation was a blessing. I looked forward to church. However, it took one day of being extremely overwhelmed, and the Pastor's words to cause me to doubt in overcoming my depression.

I walked into church. I sat on the pew with my children, and I tuned myself to listen to the Pastor preach. After listening to the message for a few minutes, I zoomed into a part of the Pastor's message: "There are some brothers and sisters that come to church two days out of the week; however, we need to come to every service!" POW! Those words punctured me deep. It is written, "Death and life are in the power of the tongue ..." (Proverbs 18:21 ESV). Yes! I absorbed the message personally into my heart.

I got up and walked out with my two children. As I drove home, I cried and said God, "I don't understand God. I am doing everything I know how. God, you know I can only come to church two days. This church is so far away. God, I am not going back to church if that is how I am going to be treated. Forget it! I am done! I am not going back!"

I did not go back to church. I continued caring for my children. I continued to follow my education goal. My daily schedule changed; it got less stressful because I was not going to church. Day after day, I felt like everything was good. I would tell myself I did not need church to change my life. My daily responsibilities kept me busy; I stopped praying, and then I even stopped talking to God. As the days went by, I had not noticed that my sweet days were becoming sour. I started complaining about not having enough money as a single mom. I complained about the daily long drives to and from my home to my children's school and to college. I complained about not having enough food. All I could see was the problems in my life.

*******NOTE*******

Today, the Lord has allowed me to understand that my heart was hurt by the Pastor's words because my spirit was vulnerable for the attacks of the enemy. I was vulnerable because my heart had not healed and I also have a sensitive Holy Spirit. I did not know to "keep [my] heart with all vigilance, for from it flow the springs of life" Proverbs 4:23 ESV) because "Death and life are in the power of the tongue ..." (Proverbs 18:21 ESV). In fact, at this moment, I hear God saying: 'Daughter I know of the pain the Pastor caused you; I know the words that caused you to walk into darkness for all those years, but I, your Father God, was always by your side.' Yes, "the Lord is near to the brokenhearted and saves the crushed in spirit" (Psalm 34:18 ESV).

As I sit here and write this piece of my life, my heart stirs up sadness, but before any anger can destroy my spirit, I hear the Lord say, "You shall not take vengeance or bear a grudge against the sons of your own people, but you shall love your neighbor as yourself; I am the Lord" (Leviticus 19:18 ESV). "As the Father has loved me, so have I loved you. Abide in my love. If you keep my commandments, you will abide in my love, just as I have kept my Father's commandments and abide in his love. These things I have spoken to you, that my joy may be in you, and that your joy may be full" (John 15:9-11 ESV), and the Lord comforted me with these words: 'Daughter, I am happy you have come back home.'

Not Ready to Wrestle

I DID NOT RETURN TO THE LORD'S CHURCH. LIVING
in a public housing apartment with my children was a blessing,
but the depression overtook my life. The lies of the enemy were
blinding me in leading me to believe that I never even needed
the Lord Jesus. I felt multiple bricks attaching to my body. One
by one, the weight of the bricks made it difficult for me to
stand tall with my head lifted high. Each brick had a name:
failure, ugly, worthless, grief, powerless, lonely, rejected, low
self-esteem, unforgiving, suicide, empty, and anger. My life was
changing right before my eyes. It is written, that "... worldly grief
produces death" (2 Corinthians 7:10 ESV).

I was running away from my depression, problems, and
pain. The devil was following me wherever I went. The devil was
having a blast twisting my loneliness into seeking Cain whom
was the big cause of my depression. I accepted and allowed Cain
to be in and out of my life as he pleased; I allowed the physical
and mental abuse to enter my life once again. Because I was not
attending church, I let my guard down. My armor and sword
were down. My spirit was not ready to wrestle! It is written,
"Put on the full armor of God [so] that you may be able to stand

against the schemes of the devil, for we do not wrestle against flesh and blood, but against the rulers, against the authorities, against the powers over ... darkness, [and] against the spiritual forces of evil ..." (Ephesians 6:11-12 ESV). I ignored my Lord and gardener of my life. The black weeds were growing in my spiritual life again. I fell back into darkness and deeper than before. Yes, I was able to function, but I was not alive!

I felt empty! Something was missing! I started going out to dancing clubs searching to fill the emptiness in me. I would drink alcohol at the clubs, and afterwards, I felt so alone! The alcohol and worldly music made me feel lonely and more deeply depressed! When I drank alcohol, I could not see the attack sneaking up on me. I had to keep watch and be alert at any strike from the devil, but to do that I had to "Be sober-minded; [to] be watchful [because] ... the devil prowls around like a roaring lion, seeking someone to devour" (1 Peter 5:8 ESV). Boy! Was I getting devoured!

I searched for more of the world to deal with my depression. This caused me to become more distanced from God's love. It is written, "Do not love the world or the things in the world. If anyone loves the world, the love of the Father is not in him. For all that is in the world – the desires of the flesh and the desires of the eyes and pride of life – is not from the Father but is from the world. The world is passing away along with its desires, but whoever does the will of God abides forever" (1 John 2:15-17 ESV).

My unwise choices buried me deeper and deeper emotionally. As a result, I would call Cain; yes, I invited danger into my life and sometimes I walked towards it. It is written, "Do not enter the path of the wicked, and do not walk in the way of the evil. Avoid it; do not go on it; turn away from it and pass on" (Proverbs 4: 14-15 ESV). The mental abuse wounded me much more than any physical abuse. The mental abuse came through the degrading words that Cain would say to me to keep me powerless. I repeated the same demeaning negative words to myself. Yes, "Death and life are in the power of the tongue ..." (Proverbs 18:21 ESV).

Because I had chosen to distant myself from my Lord Jesus, I dropped my armor and sword, and I became deaf to my Lord Jesus' voice of truth and love. Once I was my Lord's adored sheep but now I choose to go astray. It is written, Jesus says "My sheep hear my voice, and I know them, and they follow me" (John 10:27 ESV), but I had chosen to stop following, so the destructive voices came back. The demeaning voices were stronger than before I had accepted Jesus Christ. I could not silence the evil pounding negative voice in my mind. The degrading voice that belittled me! An annoying voice that followed me to bed! An irritating voice that spoke to me as I looked at the mirror! An intruding voice that dressed me up with fear and depression every morning! The persisting voice that became my shadow day and night to remind me of how worthless I felt, and how angry I felt at others and myself! I was a silent walking bomb!

I continued attending college because in college, I was able to disguise my true self. I believe I went to college because it gave me self-worth, but at the end of the day, as I walked into my home my demeanor always changed. I would force myself to finish my homework, projects, and research papers because I wanted to prove to myself that I can succeed. However, I remember a paper I wrote which described living as an underclass. I felt proud of it when I handed it in, but when it was returned to me graded with an "F", I went to the bathroom to cry. I had never received an "F" on a paper until now. It was as if I failed myself even more! I could not believe this was happening to me! To my sanity, college was a safety net that gave me purpose. I had conversations with colleagues which helped me feel less lonely. The graded papers with "A" thru "C" and the professors nice comments encouraged me, but when I got that "F", I felt that I was hit with a huge brick titled failure and pushed off the roof top of a fifth floor building!

*******NOTE*******

Today, I have learned that without my Father God, Lord Jesus, and Holy Spirit, I am a walking target. My Lord has helped me to notice that my choices in life take me towards life or death. I believe that as I functioned my Lord Jesus carried me through life. Though I gave up on seeking my Lord, he had never left me. Today, guided by my Lord Jesus' presences, I feel I have come a long way in my healing.

Focusing on my blessings, I look right through any struggles in my life. "Therefore, [I] put on the full armor of God, so that when the day of evil comes, [I] may be able to stand [my] ground. After [I] have done everything to stand, [I] stand firm with the belt of truth buckled around [my] waist [and] with the breastplate of righteousness in place, and with [my] feet fitted with the readiness that comes from the gospel of peace. In addition to all this, [I] take up the shield of faith with which [I] can extinguish all the flaming arrows of the evil one. [I] take the helmet of salvation and the sword of the Spirit which is the word of God" (Ephesians 6:13-17 NIV).

Today, I follow my Lord Jesus because I stand on his promise: "I am the light of the world. Whoever follows me will never walk in darkness, but will have the light of life" (John 8:12 NIV). Today, I conquer the negative voices as I "submit [myself]… to God. Resist the devil and he will flee from [me]" (James 4:7 NIV).

Living with an Alcoholic

LIVING WITH AN UNCONTROLLED AND ANGRY alcoholic was not what I would wish on my worst enemy. The weekends were the worst. As Friday arrived and the clock reached 5PM, my heart would beat faster and I would start pacing back and forth. I would tell myself, "Kasy, don't say a word! Kasy, if you do what you need to do, today will be a better day." I had to control my eye contact. I had to watch where I walked because I did not want to be in his way. The words "I can't", as a response to Cain, had to be deleted the second I hear the keys at the door. If I followed the restrictions I placed on my daily life, there were good days, but my good days also depended on his days. When he had a bad day, it would not matter how hard I tried to be the unresponsive doll, he always found the way to make me physically or emotionally pay for his issues.

Now, I see that Liana and Tony must have placed restrictions on their lives too. Their father yelled at me in front of them. I see now that what my children saw was traumatic. I pray every day that Liana and Tony can forgive Cain, and I pray that God reveals to them that to forgive is to heal their own hearts. I also pray that Liana and Tony can forgive me for being so weak and exposing them to all the ugly.

It was Friday. Cain wobbled in from work. The smell on him was not beer; this smell was the hard liquor, and it was so strong that he must have poured the bottle over his head and over his clothes. I served him food and placed it on the table. With a slurred, deep, and loud roaring voice, Cain shouted, "the food smells burned! Don't you know how to cook?" I tried to explain but he would not listen.

His response was not "a soft answer [that] turns away wrath, but [instead it was] a harsh word [that] stirs up anger" (Proverbs 15:1 ESV). He responded with harshness; "are you calling me a liar!" These words were my cue on what was going to happen next. I quickly whispered to Liana and Tony, "quietly walk to the room and close the door," but whispering to my children back fired. He quickly grabbed the kitchen knife and shouted "you going to ignore me and talk behind my back!" He came at us with the knife! I shouted, "Liana! Tony! Run, Run into the room!" I was running right behind them. As soon as we were in the room, I turned and slammed the door shut. Slam! The door had no way to lock it, so he was pushing the door open.

Immediately, I shouted with fear, Liana! Tony! Push your bunk bed over here! God help us!" They began to push the bunk bed, and I tried to hold the door shut as Cain stabbed with the knife and shouted on the other side of the door. The bunk bed was reaching me so I pulled as Liana and Tony pushed. The bunk bed was close to the door so I was able to swing around it and push the bunk bed. Finally, the bunk bed was barricading the door. Cain was stabbing the door with ugly words coming out of his mouth. Liana, Tony, and I dropped to the floor with our backs to the bunk bed hoping to hold back any sudden force that Cain used to push the door open. As all of us became silent, the stabbing at the door diminished, Liana and Tony fell asleep on my lap.

I cried in silence as I asked myself, "why? Why do I go back with him? Why does he treat me this way? It is written, that "husbands should love their wives as their own bodies. He who loves his wife loves himself. For no one ever hated his own flesh, but nourishes and cherishes it, just as Christ does the church" (Ephesians 5:28-29 ESV). -Cain would claim to change one day, but he would forget everything when he was drunk which was almost every day-. There was silence. I closed my eyes hoping this was all a nightmare, but then I felt a light tug on my blouse.

"Mom, I think dad left," said Liana.

"Can we move the bunk bed?" asked Tony.

"Shush, I don't know if he is gone. Wait here," I responded.

I pulled the bunk bed a little, and then I peeked through the door. I did not see him and I could not hear anything. I opened the door as far open for me to squeeze myself through and still have an opening to safely run back to if I needed.

Unwilling, I stepped out of the room. As I took another step, I heard a snore; I looked in my room and there he lay. Cain had fallen asleep. I told Liana and Tony that he was sleeping, so if they had to go to the bathroom, they needed to be quiet. We all took turns to use the bathroom. Then we ate a snack, and afterwards, I cleaned the kitchen quietly. Then all three of us went back into the children's room. I pushed the bunk bed back against the door, and I fell asleep in the children's room with them until the next morning. By the time we woke up, Cain was already gone.

*******NOTE*******

Once again, I thank God for helping my memory. Writing this piece was difficult for me. As I tried to remember that day, there were some thoughts I wanted to forget. But forgetting is nearly not possible when Liana and Tony can remember, but again, I pray they forgive his ignorance on what God says about alcohol and what it does. It is written, "Do not look at wine when it is red, when it sparkles in the [wine glass], and goes down smoothly. In the end, it bites like a serpent and stings like [a viper]. Your eyes will see strange things, and your heart utter preserve things" (Proverbs 23:31-33 ESV). With God by my side, I was able to "drive out a scoffer, and strife will go out, and quarreling and abuse will cease" (Proverbs 22:10 ESV). I know I was not a great mom with all that I put my children through because of my insecurity and depression, but I thank God he protected us through it all.

21

Jealousy Makes a Move

STILL LIVING IN PUBLIC HOUSING, I CONTINUED TO attend college. Through my college years, I seemed to build some courage in going against the demands of Cain. Our relationship was on and off which had him believing that he still held power to make rules over my decisions, but thank God I was making cracks through my shell of fear. As I started moving forward and stepping out on courage, Cain's possessive and jealous nature developed strength with an agenda to make me fall. He targeted my kindness and good will to help. Because English was my major, my cousin Tomas asked for help with his writing assignment, but my jealous ex-husband did not allow me to help my cousin with his college assignment.

So I did what I was not allowed to do. For God says, "be strong and courageous. Do not be frightened, and do not be dismayed, for the Lord your God is with you wherever you go" (Joshua 1:9 ESV). I told my cousin Tomas to meet me at the university's cafeteria. When my cousin arrived, I was working at the English department to earn my college work study grant, so I took a lunch break. Now, what happened next was only the scheme of the enemy. Because God was helping me build courage, the enemy sneaked in. I mean, throughout my college years, Cain never cared to reach me at the university and let alone call the English department.

I met up with my cousin at the university's cafeteria to tutor him on his writing. When I went back to the office, I was informed that Cain had called asking for me. To add more wood to the fire, the secretary told him I was having lunch with my cousin Thomas. The feeling of fear was not what I expected just because I wanted to help my cousin with his English paper.

Cain called me, and in an angry jealous tone, he said, "I borrowed a car from a friend and drove university! I saw your cousin exit and enter the students' parking lot! Now I see what you are doing at the university!" He slammed the phone.

As I was heading home, I did not pick up my children from my mom's home until later in the evening because I did not know what awaited me at home. When I got home, I saw the evidence that Cain had already been to the apartment. He cut the cable from the computer, and he wrote on the mirror with my red lipstick color: "stay with your cousin!" I cleaned it off and went to pick up my children, but as I returned, I was constantly checking behind me. I feared he would come from behind as he did once before. I didn't hear from him for weeks.

After two weeks, there was a knock on the door. I opened the door to find Cain holding a birthday cake for me. He apologized, and said he would change.

About a week later, he arrived home intoxicated and ranting on how I was unfaithful to him with my cousin, so I told my children to go to the room and close the door. A mixture of suppressed anger and intoxication stirs up "jealousy [and] makes a man furious, and he will not spare when he takes revenge" (Proverbs 6:34 ESV). I should have kept my mouth shut because "... a harsh word stirs up anger" (Proverbs 15:1

ESV), but instead I confronted him and I replied, "Why are you drinking alcohol? You told me that you would change." In the blink of an eye, he stepped into my personal space. He extended his right arm and had his hand opened to the wide space between his thumb and pointing finger. I saw Cain's hand coming full speed towards my neck. He lifted me up leaving my feet dangling in the air. Shocked and unable to protect myself, I felt the grasp and forceful grip around my neck. I struggled to breath. My vision blurred and still gasping for oxygen, my head became light headed and my body numb. Lights Out!

Next, I was struggling to inhale oxygen, and my mind was slowly becoming alert to my surroundings. I opened my eyes and strained to clear my vision. I could hear his intoxicated voice angrily say "that's so you'll learn!" I laid on the floor trying to absorb what happened to me. I did not know how I got there, and for how long had I been there. With an unhinged walk, he left me on the floor.

As I tried to get up, I felt dizzy. I got myself up by holding on to the wall. Then I reached for the sofa and I sat down. I inhaled and exhaled as I accepted that he had choked me unconscious. I did not sleep through the night. I sat on the sofa crying and thinking: why was I so stupid! I did not understand why I believed his apologies, and why I allow him to be in my life?

*******NOTE*******

Today, as my mind relives that moment, I hear "…my thoughts trouble me and I am distraught at the voice of the enemy, at the stares of the wicked; for they bring down suffering upon me and revile me in their anger. My heart is in anguish within me; the terrors of death assault me. Fear and trembling have beset me; horror has overwhelmed me. If an enemy were insulting me, I could endure it. If an [enemy] were rising... against me, I could hide from him. But it is you, a man, my companion, my close friend ..." (Psalm 55: 2-5, 12-13 NIV).

As I continue to write, the Lord has allowed me to hear the answers for the questions above. I accepted his apologies because I spoke negatively to myself. I believed all that happened was always my fault. I allowed him in my life because I was vulnerable, and I did not know myself worth and that I am a child of my almighty Father God. I can say once again that "... the devil prowls around like a roaring lion, seeking someone to devour" (1 Peter 5:8 ESV). I thank God for protecting me again. This could have been the end of me, but it wasn't my time.

There were years where I remembered this nightmare of my death encounter, but I now hear my Father God say, "Beloved, never avenge yourself, but leave it to the wrath of God, for it is written, 'Vengeance is mine, I will repay, says the Lord'" (Romans 12:19 ESV). During this time, I was a sheep that had slid away, but my Father God had not left me. In my crazy choices, I thank my Lord for showing me how to endure and escape my wrong choices. For it is written, "No temptation has overtaken you that is not common to man. God is faithful, and he will not let you be tempted beyond your ability, but with the temptation he will also provide the way of escape, that you may be able to endure it" (1 Corinthians 10:13 ESV).

Dream

WHEN HE WOKE UP, I MADE BELIEVE I WAS SLEEPING on the sofa. As soon as he left out the doors, I ran to the window to make sure he got in his car and drove off. I told my children to get dressed. We walked out into the hallway; then we walked down the hallway and into the elevator. I pressed the Lobby selection button. The elevator doors opened, and we walked quickly go to my car. I drove to a locksmith store and bought a door cylinder. We got in my car and drove back home. Then we retraced all of our previous steps back home, and I exchanged the door cylinder.

I packed up a bag of clothes for my children and myself. Once again, we walked out in to the hallway; then we walk down the hallway and into the elevator. I pressed the Lobby selection button. The elevator doors opened, and we walked quickly to my car. We left to my parents' home for a week. I knew Cain would be angry that his keys would no longer open the apartment door.

The morning after sleeping at my parents' home, as I walked to my car to set out to the university, I found four flat tires. The tire shop's repair man said all four tires were punctured with a knife. Because of the four punctured flat tires, I did not feel ready to return to my apartment. I concluded I had to stay at my parents' home more than a week. I figured Cain was working, so on my way to the university, I took a detour to the apartment, and I grabbed extra clothes.

I stayed at my parents for about two weeks. I slept on a full size bed with my children Liana and Tony. After a few visits to the apartment by myself, I noticed that it was safe enough to return back to the apartment with my children.

Time passed. I focused on my course assignments. I answered Cain's phone calls because he called to speak with his children, and then he wanted to speak to me. These conversations with Cain weakened me, but before I walked back into his abusive life style, I had a dream. I know God was still present in my life and trying to show me the hidden truth about Cain. God spoke to me "... in a dream" (Numbers 12:6 ESV).

In my dream, Cain, my children, and I were living together but then there was someone knocking on the door. I opened the door and there was a lady that said, "Is Cain there? I'm here to let him know that we are having a problem with our marriage license." Cain got up from the chair and as he walked out with this lady, he looked at me with a worried look. Then I woke up.

Now, before I continue with the dream, let me remind you that I had divorced him a few years earlier. We were still living together on and off, and he had not mentioned any changes in his relationship commitments.

A few days later, as I searched for a confirmation to the dream, I asked him to meet me at the park so I can speak to him. Then I was led to do reverse psychology on Cain, but let me fill you in on a secret. Cain always thought my family hand a lot of money, and this perception of me helped with the reverse psychology. I started with putting on my sun glasses because my eyes speak when I'm not saying the truth.

"Are you married?" I asked.

"No," he responded.

"Again, are you married?" I asked again.

"Why are you asking?" He asked.

"I already know the truth but I want to hear it from you." I responded.

"What do you know?" He asked.

"Again, the cost wasn't a problem for me and I know the truth, but I want to hear it from you." I answered.

As he reached for my sun glasses, he demanded, "Take off your sun glasses!"

From an impulse, I submerged my head to his risen hand. I quickly lifted my head displaying courage. I repeated my question, "Are you married?"

After a few minutes of silence, "Yes, but I don't love her," Cain answered.

Though I thought I had prepared myself for his answer, I became silent. I focused to connect the dream God had allowed me to see to the answer that confirmed it all. The message God gave me was real! As I absorbed, I also noticed that the reverse psychology worked. With mixed emotions, I finally responded, "You know something? It didn't cost me a penny and you just told me all I needed to know!"

*******NOTE*******

Today, I see that God still loved me even though I had stopped going to church. My Father God was giving me the courage to step out and change the cylinder of the door. As I faced my fear, God said "Fear not, for I am with you; be not dismayed, for I am your God; I will strengthen you; I will help you, [and] I will uphold you with my righteous right hand" (Isaiah 41:10 ESV).

Simultaneously, because I did not have a true relationship with my Lord Jesus, I was vulnerable to the serpents' tricks, so God allowed me to see Cain's hidden life through a dream.

23

Fight, Focus, and Achievement

I CONTINUED PURSUING MY COLLEGE EDUCATION, and I focused on raising my children Liana and Tony. Day after day, my college courses became difficult but I held on. My challenges were daily. It was not easy to shuffle being a single mom, college student, working in the university's English department to earn a stipend, and student teaching. I thank God because I held on to the fight over depression, so I could focus on what had to get done.

Yes, there were ups and downs. The years of holding strong were heavy, but I know now God kept an eye on me even though I gave up on him. It was God that got me up in the mornings to get my children and myself ready for our day's agenda. I know now it was my Father God that had comforted me during the nights because I was too depressed to sleep or to even look forward to wake up in the mornings. It was God that helped me complete all the courses and assignments required towards my goal.

After 10 years, which include the years I stopped attending college because of my medical health and maternity, it was finally the year 2000, and I was about to become a CUNY graduate. The graduation was held on the university's field. The sun beam toasted my cheeks making them as red as tomatoes. My parents, my sisters Olivia and Sophia, my brother David, my cousin Amy, and my children Liana and Tony were present to cheer me on as my name was called to receive my bachelor's degree.

As I walked up to the stage to receive my bachelor of arts, the trials of my life flashed through my eyes. I could not believe I made it. Even though the ugly in my life was from my choices, I thank God for his mercy and grace. It was only with God's mercy and grace that I was able to complete a major in the English language and minor in elementary education. But yes, even in this joyous moment the enemy turned it into failure. As I sat looking at the students that graduated with a 3.0 GPA, I heard that negative voice that said, "You only have a 2.89 GPA." Then the sun's heat pierced my left hand and woke me from the negative patronizing words.

Afterwards, I went to school to take pictures with the principal and my colleagues that supported me with my student teaching. I was a parent in the same school where my son Tony attended. As I took pictures, I searched for courage on how to ask the principal for a position at the school. I searched and searched for bravery, but I could not bring myself to be that bold. Though I graduated, I wanted to volunteer as a student teacher till the end of the school year, so I told myself I will try to be bolder and ask the principal the following day.

I ended my special day with a surprise party at my parents' home where all my family was present to join me in my achievement. I was the first one of my family to receive a bachelor's degree.

Yes, my celebration was awesome until I saw Cain. My mind zoomed through all my hard times; then fear and anger tried to pry open my feelings and steal my joy again, but this time there would be no sun heat to wake me up from the negative thoughts. I know it was God that helped me keep my thoughts and feelings under control "for God gave [me] a spirit not of fear but of power and love and self-control" (2 Timothy 1:7 ESV). I did not allow fear to ruin my day, so I enjoyed every moment. I laughed. I talked about my future goals with my family. I ate cake and smiled. I did not allow myself to be tormented by Cain's presences. I took advantage of this wonderful day because I felt like I finally did something right. I was the center of attention. I had a sweet evening during my graduation celebration. I did not want this evening to end.

*******NOTE*******

Today, I want to thank God for using the sun to wake me from the enemy's lie about my GPA and for redirecting my thoughts to focus and enjoy my special day. It is written "Be strong and courageous. Do not fear or be in dread of them, for it is the lord your God who goes with you. He will not leave you or forsake you" (Deuteronomy 31:6 ESV). My Lord continues to guide my heart towards the "fruit of the Spirit [which] is love, joy, peace, patience, kindness, goodness, faithfulness, gentleness, [and] self-control; [for] against such things there is no law" (Galatians 5:22-23 ESV). I was able to fight my obstacles and wrong choices, stay focused, and achieve my goal because of God's love, grace, and mercy for me. I was able to enjoy my blessed achievement.

God Loved Me First

THE BRIGHT SUNNY MORNING GLARED THROUGH my window shades. As I woke up, my eyes got fixated on my graduation gown that hanged in my half opened closet. Did it really happen? I got out of bed and went to the bathroom to wash my face and teeth. I walked back to my room and stood in front of the mirror dresser, and as I looked down to get the hair brush, my eyes fixated on my bachelor's degree. It was not a dream! I had completed college! I was a CUNY graduate! After all my trails and challenges, God took me through it! I made it! Yes, tears of joy.

My career goal was just beginning. Now, I needed to get hired as a teacher. I told my children to get ready for school, and I got dressed. I walked to the car with my children, and we first drove to Liana's middle school. I took my daughter to her classroom line up. Then I went to the school where I did student teaching and where Tony attended classes. Though I had graduated, I wanted to continue volunteering until the end of the school year. I walked into the school, and I sent Tony to go line up with his class. As I walked to the Principal's office,

I reminded myself of the courage I needed to ask the Principal for a position.

As I went into the office to sign my name in the volunteer book, my heart's beat went fast. My mind went through different scenarios on how to ask the principal for a position. Then I heard, "Ms. Heart. The Principal is requesting to see you in her office," said the secretary quickly. I stood up straight as my mind searched for the right words to request for a position. My years of college courses flashed like a bolt of lightning through my mind as I prepared myself for any question. In the search, I also looked for a course that would have taught me on how to inquire for a position, but I could not find any preparedness course for what I needed. In my inner voice, I called on to God; "please God help me get hired." I reached for the door knob, and I took a deep breath in and exhaled; I turned the knob and opened the door. I walked in.

"Good Morning," I greeted with a smile.

"Good Morning, Ms. Heart. Once again, I would like to congratulate you on your success," Principal Mrs. Parker greeted in return.

"Thank you," I responded.

"Ms. Heart; what was it that you studied?" Principal Mrs. Parker asked.

"I received a Bachelor of Arts; my major is in the English Language and my minor is Elementary Education," I responded.

I had the opportunity to reply to a position! I should have said something, but I did not say a word. I believe God had just opened the door of continued success, but I just closed it! I was disappointed with myself.

"Ms. Heart, through your student teaching year with us, I have seen your fresh skills, love for teaching our children, and creativity in the classroom. Therefore, I know that you will be a great addition to our staff of teachers, so would you like to stay with us?" Revealed Principal, Mrs. Parker.

"Yes, I would love to be part of the staff and school. Thank you for the opportunity," I responded with a smile from cheek to cheek.

"Great. See the secretary and she will inform you on the additional steps you need to take to be ready for the new school year in September. Have a wonderful day," closing words of Principal, Mrs. Parker.

"Again, thank you," I responded still in a silent shock. I turned myself over to the door, reached for the door knob, turned it, opened the door, walked out, and closed the door behind me.

I just got hired! Wow, God helped me. Why? I had accepted Jesus as my Lord and savior but I had stop going to church, and I did not read my Bible. Now, I asked God to help me and God blesses me. Though the question remained in my mind, I took the blessing and continued to the classroom to help. The rest of my day was beautiful. When the 3PM bell rang, I helped the classroom teacher with the dismissal of 26 students. I got Tony from his class line up, and we went to the office. I signed out, wished everyone a good evening, and walked out of the building. As we walked to the car, I repeated to myself, "God helped me. Why?"

*******NOTE*******

As I wrote this piece, my mind tries to make sense of this, and here is my understanding. Yes, I stopped going to church, but I still believed and loved Father God and Jesus. Now, I am not saying that going to church is not needed because I would be so wrong. The Pastors are placed by God to feed us the Holy Words of the Bible and teach us on how to have a relationship with our Lord. The relationship with my Lord is what I lacked, so going to an anointed church that can help you through your walk and the healing process is a must. As I continue to write my understanding of God's blessing, I hear the words, "God is Love."

There is my answer! God still loved me even though I had walked out of church when spoken words hurt me. God blessed me so that today I can see that he had never given up on me.

I "... have come to know and to believe the love that God has for us. God is love, and whoever abides in love abides in God, and God abides in him" (1 John 4:16 ESV). God reminds me of his deep love thru his blessings because even though I didn't deserve it, God's love is more than any human can repay. "For God so loved the world, that he gave his only Son, that whoever believes in him shall not perish but have eternal life" (John 3:16 NIV). "God shows his love for us in that while we were still sinners, Christ died for us" (Romans 5:8 ESV).

God loved me, so he was teaching me by example. It is written, "Love is patient and kind; love does not envy or boast; it is not arrogant or rude. It does not insist on its own way; it is not irritable or resentful; it does not rejoice at wrongdoing, but rejoices with the truth. Love bears all things, believes all things, hopes all things, [and] endures all things. Love never ends ..." (1 Corinthians 13:4-8 ESV). God was showing his love and that he will wait patiently for my return to the first love where I accepted his only Son Jesus Christ. God wanted to remind me that "... he first loved [me]" (1 John 4:19 NIV).

In this chapter, I see and thank God now for what I did not notice in my past. The Lord's blessing were pouring on me because "... he first loved [me]" (1 John 4:19 NIV). God blessed me so that today I can see that he had never given up on me. As a human, I have made many mistakes. I have sinned. As a victim of domestic violence, I lost faith and doubted on God's help for my life. I walked out of God's temple because of man. But today, my Father God has allowed me to see and understand how much he loves me. Though I will have ups and downs as a human, God's "Love is patient and kind" (1 Corinthians 13:4 ESV). "... God is Love ..." (1 John 4:16 ESV).

God loved me first as he woke me up with oxygen. God loved me because he allowed me to see the sun's glare through my window. God allowed me to see and experience the good feeling of achievement as I saw my graduation gown and my bachelor's degree. He continued to love me as he told the Principal Mrs. Parker to give me a position as a teacher in the school.

God loves me even more because he is guiding my fingers as I write this book. My Father God's love for me never ends.

Shouts of Joy

THE SUMMER MONTHS OF JULY AND AUGUST WENT by quickly. The New York School District became the place most visited by me. I gathered my transcript, completed criminal background check, FBI finger print check, child abuse clearance, and any other credential paperwork requested. I had been hired as a per diem teacher. As a per diem teacher, I was given a three year period to complete and achieve the teacher licensing test. By the end of August, I completed the steps need to prepare me to begin teaching by September 2000.

Besides getting prepared to begin work in September, I had to make some changes for me, Liana and Tony's living arrangements. We had to move out of the public housing apartment because based on my income the rent was going to increase from $300 to $800 a month. The apartment was worth the rent increase. However, the stench of urine in the hallway and elevator and the unsafe location of the building were not worth the rent, so I moved back to my parents' home in Brooklyn. At the end, it all worked out because Liana and Tony had already been attending school in Brooklyn because

I did not approve of the zoned schools for the public housing apartment.

We settled our things in the first floor apartment. This was a two bedroom apartment. My father and I with my children shared the apartment. My father slept in one room, and my daughter slept in the other room. My son Tony and I used the big spaced living room which I divided into three sections. One section for Tony, another me, and a living room section. We shared the kitchen and bathroom with my father.

Liana was in middle school. Tony was in elementary school which was the same school where I was hired. It all came together. I was going from one part of my life to another. "For everything, there is a season and a time for every matter under heaven" (Ecclesiastes 3:1 ESV).

I moved on with my life. My children's father would visit them, but thank God I felt stronger as to not fall in his trap of confusion. I focused on my children and on my new career as an educator. Yes, I was happy! It is written that "those who sow in tears shall reap with shouts of joy!" (Psalm 126:5 ESV). The night before my first day of work, I said my prayers and fell asleep.

Buzz, Buzz, Buzz, echoed the alarm clock. As I opened my eyes, I hit the off button on the alarm clock. I stood in bed a few minutes, and I wondered if I had been dreaming. Was this really my first day of work? Yes! It was the first day of school for teachers only. I got dressed, ate a light breakfast, and drove to the school. As I walked into the school building office, I was greeted with smiles and good mornings by the principal and other staff members.

Then I received the keys of my assigned classroom. I was in unbelief. I walked towards the classroom door. I unlocked the door to the classroom, opened the door, and let myself inside.

I organized and prepared the classroom for the first day of school for the children. I was assigned first grade. I finished the classroom preparations, and as I walked out the classroom, I looked over my right shoulder and pictured the empty seats filled with children. I posted my name "Ms. Heart" outside the classroom door, and my eyes got watery with joy.

My first year as a teacher was challenging. I tried to find solutions to manage behavior issues like write anecdotes on children that needed extra help. I prepared lesson plans, graded children's class work, homework, and exams. I updated bulletin boards, and stayed in contact with parents on their children's progress. The blessing of being an educator minimized any challenges I faced in the classroom.

*******NOTE*******

Wow, today I thank God for all he has allowed me to see. I was hired before I could ask for a position. The living arrangements changed once again, but by this time I noticed that with God at the wheel every stop is temporary. I see now that moving back to my parents' home was more like a blessing than a step backwards. My parents' home was the transportation terminal; I had already received the teaching career which was the ticket for my transfer, but now I had to wait on God to direct me to the next shuttle. "The heart of man plans his way, but the Lord establishes his steps" (Proverbs 16:9 ESV).

God, Have Mercy on Our Nation!

THE NEW SCHOOL YEAR 2001 BEGAN. THIS YEAR I was assigned second grade on the second floor. I knew this year would be much better because I had gained experience in a classroom by myself in the first year. Throughout the summer, I had collected children's books from family and some I bought at discount prices from the library and book banks. I brought new ideas. I organized the classroom to accommodate the balance literacy learning curriculum.

The balance literacy curriculum's appearance gave the children a feeling like if they were in their homes, so as to feel less stress. The children were grouped into small reading group which met with me as the other groups took turns in different learning centers. I had a two seat sofa, a coffee table, throw pillows, and no teacher's desk which gave the classroom an appearance of being a large room. The first week mostly consisted of reviewing classroom rules, getting to know the children's names and development reading assessment levels, and walking quietly in a line from one destination to the other.

"Good morning children," I said.

"Good morning Ms. Heart," responded the children.

"Please unpack your backpacks and quietly put them in the closet and begin your journal writing," I instructed.

Time Passed. "Ok children, journal writing is over. Put your notebooks in your desk and walk quietly to the rug," I instructed.

After the morning message, shared reading, and guided reading was completed, we had to get ready to go to Science class, so I instructed the boys; "Boys quietly line up."

After the boys were lined up, I then instructed the girls; "Now, girls can you line up quietly?"

The children were lined up. "Awesome! I love how quiet everyone lined up. We are ready to open the door and walk quietly in the hallway as we go to science class," I said.

I opened the door. Anguish defied me face to face. I did not understand what I was feeling. I peeked out into the hallway to check for other classes and further down the hallway there were two teachers walking and in tears. As they approached my classroom, they turned their faces away from the students so that they could not see the teachers' sorrow and tears. An empty hallway screaming with cries of anguish, and the teachers with tears of sorrow infused my soul. Why? What was going on? I did not understand.

"Line leaders, please walk up to our first stop," I instructed. The children walked out and lined up in the hallway, and I closed the classroom door. I walked up to the front of the line which was the corner of the hallway before the children turned. As I stood in front, I commended the children for such a nice job. Then I looked to make sure the hallway was clear for the children to turn the corner and proceed. I saw two other teachers in tears. They quickly turned their faces away from the children, and they opened the staircase doors and walked through. I felt the sorrow but I did not understand.

"Line leaders, please walk up to the science classroom door," I instructed once more. I walked up to the science classroom. The door was opened, so I looked inside to ask the teacher if she was ready to receive the children. She was at her desk and in tears, too.

"Are you, ok?" I asked.

The science teacher walked over to me, and as she dried her tears, she asked, "Didn't you hear?"

"No. What happened?" I responded.

With watery eyes, the science teacher said, "Two airplanes hit the Twin Towers."

I froze in shock and my whole body became numb with tears in my eyes. Then I was able to speak, "What can I do? Do I take the children back to class?"

"No, I will stay with the children, and I know help is needed downstairs," responded the science teacher.

"Ok," I answered.

As I took the steps towards downstairs, I feared for Liana and Tony's safety, so I quickly searched my pocket for my flip phone. I called my dad and told him to pick up Liana at the middle school, and then to come and pick up Tony. I explained to my dad to call me when he was near so that I can call Tony's teacher to have him sent to my classroom. After I finished speaking to my dad, I closed my flip phone, placed it in my pocket, and I tried not to break down in tears before I opened the door leading to the first floor.

I opened the door leading to the first floor. There were so many crying and fearful parents wanting to pick up their children. All the staff was helping in the reunion of children with their parents. As I helped, there was one moment that I will never forget. I went to a kindergarten class room; I called out the young girl's name and then the little girl asked, "Did I do something wrong?"

"No baby. You haven't done anything wrong," I responded. We walked down the hallway, and immediately, the mother ran up to her daughter and hugged her tightly.

"I love you," said the mother.

"I love you, mom," responded the little girl.

I returned to the classroom with my children. My son and daughter were picked up by my dad, and one by one the children of my classroom were picked up, too. By three o'clock, there were about eight children remaining to be picked up. When the last child was picked up, I was able to leave.

I went home. When I walked into the house, my parents were watching the news as it replayed the Twin Towers being hit and falling. This was my first time watching what had happened on the television. It was Tuesday, September 11, 2001, and we were in a State of emergency! On the television, the news reporter informed the public of many emergency responders: firemen and police officers that were trapped under the rubbles, and as a result, we worried about my brother David because he was a New York police officer. But our worries were placed at ease when my brother walked in. I walked up to him and asked him, "Don't you work today?"

And he responded, "No. Today is my day off, but I did call the precinct and asked if I had to report to work, but I was told that I should report tomorrow for the second shift." At this moment, I knew it was God's love who had kept my brother David from that danger.

*******NOTE*******

As I wrote the chapter, I remember this day was a nightmare. I pray for the comforting of the hearts of the families that lost loved ones in this horrific terrorist attack on the Twin Towers of New York City and other parts of the United States. The United States had been infiltrated by the enemy and we did not see it coming. I thank God that my family and I are still here to tell of his mercy because "it [was] the Lord who [went and continues to go] before [us]; he will not leave [us] or forsake [us] …" (Deuteronomy 31:8 ESV). At this moment, without understanding, it is ironic how the numbers 911 which is our emergency call number is now also a memory to the horrific terrorist attack of 9/11.

God gives everyone mercy; however, what I see now is that for a long time the United States has been taking God out of our Judeo-Christian values, and allowing and accepting non-Christian values. I believe that when the United States pulled the Bible out of the public schools, they opened the door to evil. It is written, "Be careful to keep the commandment and the law that Moses the servant of the Lord gave you, to love the Lord your God, to walk in all his ways, to obey his commands, to hold fast to him and to serve him with all your heart and with all your soul" (Joshua 22:5 NIV).

God has been warning the United States in his Holy Bible: "Do not love the world or the things in the world. If anyone loves the world, the love of the Father is not in him. For all that is in the world –the desires of the flesh and the desires of the eyes and pride of life–is not from the Father but is from the world. And the world is passing away along with its desires, but whoever does the will of God abides forever" (1 John 2: 15-17 ESV). In Psalm 46:10 (ESV), God has also raised his voice to say, "Be still, and know that I am God. I will be exalted among the nations. I will be exalted in the earth!" God is merciful but are we the United States under his merciful love or are we falling away?

Fear of the End

THE DAY AFTER THE HORRIFIC TERRORIST ATTACK on the Twin Towers, Pentagon, and the heroes of flight United 93 that did not let their airplane reach the third target Washington, DC, I found myself reliving the terrorist attacks. I had tears and heartaches for all the lives lost on that day. There were innocent lives taken on those airplanes. There were innocent lives in the Twin Towers, flight United 93, and the Pentagon. All the people that jumped from the Twin Towers' windows for reasons they only knew. The day our nation came to a standstill. The day we waited for another attack. I could not stop thinking that we were all going to die! The end was pushing on the door!

Yes, I felt the end was here. The fear of what I had seen and the fear of the unknown led me back into the arms of my abuser. After a few years of walking with more confidence in myself, I stepped back into my past. I went back with him. Cain and I came together for a few days like if it was our last day. It wasn't long until all was as it had been. Nothing had really changed. He was still an alcoholic. He was still possessive. He was still abusive.

It wasn't long before I was pregnant. Technology had

upgraded so much that I requested to know my baby's gender. It's a Boy! I told him that I was having a baby, but his response was not a joyous one. Although Cain was not on board with a baby's arrival, I lifted my head up high and said "I will have this baby! I don't want to hear your alternative. I was stupid twice before but I thank God that I am stronger now. I have faith that with my teaching career I will be able to raise my three children alone!" I was shocked at the words that came out of my mouth. It was God that gave me that boldness and strength to stand up to my abuser. Wow, though I had left my Christian walk, God was still reminding me of his Holy Word where it is written, "Have I not commanded you? Be strong and courageous. Do not be frightened, and do not be dismayed, for the Lord your God is with you wherever you go" (Joshua 1:9 ESV).

Pregnant and getting up in the mornings to teach second grade students, it was not easy, but I was not going to give up now. My body had to adapt to working while pregnant because when I was pregnant with Liana and Tony I was home. Now I was pregnant, working, and watching and teaching about 30 second grade children. I could not stop crying at nights as I feared on how I was going to raise three children on my own and still living in my parents' home. This fear was just another lie of the enemy because if God had carried me this far, as I overcame so much, why would God leave me now? "For God gave [me] a spirit not of fear but of power and love and self-control" (2 Timothy 1:7 ESV), and "I can do all things through [Christ] who strengthens me" (Philippians 4:13 ESV).

Though I tried to stay emotionally stress free, I did the total opposite. When I was four months pregnant, I felt the symptoms of having a miscarriage. I drove myself to the emergency room, but as I drove, I cried and prayed:

"God, I'm sorry for the two abortions in my past. I'm sorry

for worrying on how I would be able to care for my children. I allowed myself to be led by fear, insecurity, and in search of a companion and love. God, I still remember when I was pregnant with Tony and how Cain would visit but to ask about Tony but not about me! God, that was painful in my heart. After Tony was born nothing changed because Cain continued with the alcohol and abusing me mentally and physically. God, who ever said having a baby will fix a relationship must have not consulted with you. God, I have fallen in love with my baby boy; please God, don't let me loose the baby."

I arrived at the hospital. As I got out of the car, I felt the symptom of a miscarriage get worse. I walked into the emergency room and was seen immediately. The gynecologist checked me and told me I had to be at bed rest plus he emphasized that I could not stress, worry, or lift heavy stuff for two weeks. The doctor added that if I continued bleeding, they would have to do an abortion.

I went home. The next morning, I sent my dad to the school with the excuse note for two weeks. The note was to be given to the principal. I remained bed rest for two weeks. My two children and family helped me, but I could not stop crying and worrying. Those two weeks were the longest worries ever! I know I was supposed to be relaxed, but I could not stop crying myself to sleep at night. After the two weeks of bed rest, I noticed I wasn't bleeding anymore. I was thanking God for his mercy and grace in allowing me to keep my baby boy. Wow, God still loved me because even though I had stopped going to church, God had mercy on me.

I continued working as a teacher with about 30 second grade children. This pregnancy was different because I did not have a full time job when I was pregnant with Liana and Tony. It was a challenge working full time and pregnant. At the eighth month,

I got very emotional. I took maternity leave two weeks prior to the day I had set out to leave. Now, because of my history of the severe asthma and being diagnosed with gestational diabetes, the doctor labeled me a high risk pregnancy.

My unborn baby was not able to arrive into the world on the due date. The doctor sent me to get induced labor but that did not work either, so I was sent back home. A week later, I was told by the doctor to admit myself to the hospital to do a C-Section delivery. My youngest sister Sophia accompanied me to the hospital, and she helped me decide on a name. My baby's name came from the listing of names on the credits after a movie on the television. Yes, in pain, and trying to decide on a name. Thank God, I carried my baby boy to full term, and his name is Brian!

*******NOTE*******

Today, I feel God say that September 11[th's] attack was a day that everyone feared and many thought it was the End of the world. I believe many people must have searched for the presences of God. It is written, we should have "sought the LORD, and he [would have] … delivered [us] from all [our] fears" (Psalm 34:4 ESV). Likewise, many made other choices. Some ran towards the alcohol. Some took their own lives. Some ran to their family and others ran towards their spouses. Nothing is wrong with running towards the family but together seek the Lord Jesus for comfort and security.

Yes, God told me that where I should have run to on that day was to his temple. It is written, "When I am afraid, I [should] put my trust in [God]" (Psalm 56:3 ESV). God has also revealed that the reason I did not run to his church was because I was lost in the world. When I went to church, I knew and felt I was the daughter of God. I knew the church was my home away from home. It was the place I felt safe and loved by God. However, when I stopped attending church, it was like I had ran away from home, and as a runaway, I felt lost and confused in this time of fear and devastation. It was difficult to go back home to the church because I was lost in the world's pain.

Lost in the world's pain, I ran blindly into the arms of another lost soul. I understand now that after seeing all those lives from the Twin Towers have no escape, I really did not see my past abusive relationship being that bad any more. I wanted comfort and to feel secured even if it was in the arms of my abusive ex-husband. In the mist of all the darkness, God blessed me. I thank God for giving me the blessing of having my baby boy Brian.

28

Leap of Faith

BEFORE THE YEAR 2002 ENDED, I HAD VOWED TO BUY a house for me and my three children. I did not want to continue living in my parents' home. I had to take a "leap of faith." I figured I had a teacher's salary of about $30,000, good credit score, and a $6,000 deposit.

In November, I made an appointment with three different realtors. I went prepared with all I could possibly need for the process of buying a house. However, each realtor said, my income was not enough for any house in any part of New York because the prices were ranging over $200,000. They suggested renting an apartment, but with my monthly income, I was not able to manage a $1,500 rent, plus utilities, and regular needs. I went to my parents' home with no hope of ever having a house to call home for me and my children.

Yes, at bed time, I cried and spoke to God because it is written, "… whatever [I] ask in prayer, [I] will receive, if [I] have faith" (Matthew 21:22 ESV), so I asked, "God, will I ever be able to buy a house for me and my children? God, now it is three children. God, I cannot continue raising my children living altogether in a 30'L x 12'W space. God, I'm sorry I don't pray often but I'm asking you for help." I closed my eyes, tears slide down my cheeks, and I fell asleep.

The following morning was a Saturday, and without having planned it, I left my children with my mom, and I drove to Philadelphia in search of a house. On the first drive to Philadelphia, I saw three houses between the price ranges of $51,000 to $70,000, and I chose the $51,000 house. The realtor used my teacher's salary from the two years of working in New York. I really did not ask many questions because I was happy I was buying a house. I mailed a check for $1,000 for the processing of the papers for purchasing the house. In the beginning of the year 2003, I signed the closing papers and wrote the final check for $5,000. My mortgage was $432 a month for a three bedroom and one bathroom single family home. I bought a house in Philadelphia. Yes, the house needed some work, but my dad took care of that because every weekend he went to Philadelphia and fixed the house.

Now, I want to highlight how the Lord watched over me. After I purchased my house, I was given lay-off papers at my school because I had not been able to pass the L.A.S.T which was a requirement to become a licensed teacher in New York, so my last month teaching was June 2003. After my last day of work, I applied for my unemployment and gave my new address. Yes, I packed up my things and gathered my three children. As I drove on to the New Jersey Turnpike towards our new home, there were tears in my eyes because I had been born and raised in Brooklyn, New York. After so much physical and mental abuse, I had finally collected and secured all my sparks of courage to move forward. Yes, as single mom with three children, I moved to Philadelphia.

*******NOTE*******

God wrote my story the day I was born, and though I had constantly caused him to re-write my life story, at the end, my almighty Father God had been filling me with hope and courage every time I left Cain. God revealed that though it is written, "wives, submit to your husbands as to the Lord" (Ephesians 5:22 ESV). It is also written, that "husbands, love your wives, as Christ loved the church and gave himself up for her" (Ephesians 5:25 ESV). I trust and believe that God never meant for wives to stay in a relationship where they get physically and mentally abused. I believe that no one should remain in a physical or mental abusive relationship. Yes, the vow says till death do you apart, but I also have read that the man should be an example of a righteous husband in the home by showing the Lord Jesus' love. It is written, "In this same way, husbands should love their wives as their own bodies. He who loves his wife loves himself" (Ephesians 5:28 ESV). Here it is, husbands that beat or mentally abuse their wives do not love themselves, so how can they show their wives love! Again, this is what I have concluded. We need to recognize the difference between a covenant and submission of a wife that lives in fear from domestic abuse. God loved me, and he led me to see myself worth.

God never gave up on me. As I searched my soul for strength, the Lord Jesus led me to collect and secure all my sparks of courage, and he guided me to Philadelphia with hope for a new beginning. For it is written, "'I know the plans I have for you', declares the LORD, 'plans for welfare and not for evil, to give you a future and a hope'" (Jeremiah 29:11 ESV).

I thank God for answering my prayers and guiding me to Philadelphia. It is written, "The heart of man plans his way, but the Lord establishes his steps" (Proverbs 16:9 ESV). Only God knew where I had to go to find the right price home, but most of all, God had the house buying process go smoothly and be completed before I was laid off.

Thank you God for the oxygen I inhale and for the strength you have given me to overcome my trails. Thank you God because as I battled through all the trials in my life, you were there through every step. Thank you, Father God for your love and mercy that allows me to say today: "I'm Alive!"

Author's Letter to the Reader

Dear Reader,

As I finished writing this book, I hear God saying to me, "Daughter, I saw and dried all your tears. I know about the mental and physical abuse you endured. I forgive you for the two abortions. Daughter, I am proud of you for not giving up on yourself. I am proud of your accomplishments and remember to continue your prayers."

Through this journey of my life, I was given the blessing to accept Jesus in my heart and be baptized, but because of the lies of the enemy, I stopped seeking God's love. My relationship with the Lord had static which caused bumps in my life. Though there were a lot of downs, my Lord found the time and place where he blessed and advanced me. Yes, the road had many bumps and most of them very high ones, but God was not going to let any bump or hill stop me and keep me from his plan for my life. God is so merciful that he never stopped loving me. Though I had not known the Holy Word in the beginning, and then after knowing the Lord Jesus, I walked away, the Lord always loved me first.

Today, I am proud to say that I am a faithful daughter of the almighty God. I'm a Christian! I also want to say that I wrote this book because it is written, "Go home to your friends and tell them how much the Lord has done for you, and how he has had mercy on you" (Mark 5:19 ESV), and "If I alone bear witness about myself, my testimony is not deemed true" (John 5:31 ESV).

I lived in a domestic abusive relationship for 13 years, and I did not know if I would see the next day. Thanks to the Lord, I walked away in June 2003, and yes it has not been peaches and cream raising my three children on my own, but I am still alive!

God has led me to write my testimony so that you can understand that we first need to love and have a relationship with the Lord. The Lord can guide us out of a painful and abusive relationship. The Lord can forgive our sins. The Lord can give us courage in moving forward. Yes, the Lord gave me courage to take the leap of faith to be a single mom with three children.

"We know that for those who love God all things work together for good for those whom are called according to his purpose" (Romans 8:28 ESV).

Sister in Christ Jesus,

Kasy Heart

God Bless You Always
I pray to be the light where there is darkness and the voice where there has been silence too long.

References

NIV Adventure Bible, Revised, New International Version. Copyrights 1989, 1994, 2000, 2008. Grand Rapids, Michigan by Zonderkidz

The Holy Bible, English Standard Version. ESV. Permanent text Edition 2016. Copyrights 2001, By Crossway. BibleGateway. www.biblegateway/versions/english-standard-version-ESV-Bible/#booklist.com

Printed in the United States
By Bookmasters